The Cursed Secret Tomb

Farah Uddin

Copyright © 2024 Farah Uddin

All rights reserved.

ISBN: 979-8-3043-3259-0

For my Uddin 3 and a special thanks to Ms. Peach.

CONTENTS

ACKNOWLEDGMENTS i

Chapter One 3

Chapter two 15

Chapter three 39

Chapter four 49

Chapter five 68

Chapter six 76

Chapter seven 80

Chapter eight 89

Chapter nine 105

Chapter ten 112

Chapter eleven 122

Chapter thirteen 144

Chapter fourteen 154

Chapter fifteen 164

ABOUT THE AUTHOR 169

ACKNOWLEDGMENTS

Writing this book was a very new journey for me, my first book aimed at my young readers. What used to be bedtime stories for my children, are slowly being turned into stories for all children. I hope everyone enjoys reading this book as much as I enjoyed writing it. Also, a special mention with love and thanks to my husband for his support, encouragement and help.

PROLOGUE

The priests from the Temple of Ma'at stayed silent as they made their way back to the temple. They had agreed to never speak of this night or of their actions ever again. Amongst them was a young boy, who had only recently joined the ranks of priesthood, his hands still shook from having held down the Pharaoh as they cursed him. He could still feel the power that had been in that tomb, the dark and negative energy.

He desperately needed to make sense of it all, but having been forbidden from speaking about it, the only thing he could do was to write it all down on a scroll.

With a shaky hand he wrote the following; Tonight a very dark deed took place. We the priests of Ma'at managed to rid the world of the traitor, Pharaoh Nakht-Ankh. Many years ago, our beloved Pharaoh Amunotep was betrayed by his most trusted advisor, Nakht-Ankh. In his greed for the throne, he killed Amunotep and declared himself Pharaoh.

He was cruel to the people, he was greedy, laying his hands on all the gold he could. Amunotep's loyal guards came to us with a plan to overthrow him.

For his crimes, Nakht-Ankh was sentenced to death. We cursed his tomb, trapping his spirit, placing all the treasures he had touched in his tomb, out of his reach and cursed like him. Those treasures would only bring ill fate to anyone who coveted them like he had.

We did not honour this tomb with a name, instead placed a warning on it: 'Stay away from this place. Those who enter will share in the cursed one's fate, forever guarding the treasures they seek.'

Once this was all written, the young priest rolled up the scroll and hid it beneath a loose stone in the floor of his room. Finally, he was able to lay down, but sleep did not come, he had a sinking feeling that his part in this curse would haunt him for the rest of his life.

Chapter One

Theo tried to concentrate on his homework, but right now it was just a tiny bit difficult because the TV was blaring in the background while his sister held their dad hostage as she did his hair. Becki was 6 years old, and her favourite thing to do was play with people's hair. Every now and then he heard them shout, 'Is it cake?' as the people on TV cut into real looking objects that turned out to be cake.

He looked over at his grandpa Harold, due to being bald he was never selected as Becki's hair model, lucky him. Right now, his grandpa was sitting in his favourite armchair by the window, reading another history book. He had a huge interest in ancient Egypt, just like his own father, Theodore, and grandfather, Reginald, had before him. The history bug had clearly skipped Theo's dad, James Hawthorne, who was an accountant.

Theodore Hawthorne, (Not Theo, in case anyone wondered, but Theo's great grandpa, the man that Theo had been named after), had gone missing on his first and only excavation, that's what they call digging for ancient relics.

Putting his pen down he went over to his grandpa and pulled a stool out to sit next to Harold, 'What you reading today grandpa? Anything interesting?'

Harold looked up, his eyes twinkling, always happy to share about history, 'Ooh it's a good one today my boy' he told Theo excitedly.

'I don't think I have yet told you about Pharaohs and their tombs. Well, did you know that when Pharaohs got buried, they often had more than one chamber in their tombs?'

'Isn't that them just wasting extra space that they don't need?' he asked.

'They thought they needed it Theo, you see, Pharaohs were always very rich, and they believed that they would need their treasures in their afterlife, so they horded it and had it buried with them. But, to throw off any thieves, they usually had several chambers in their tombs to confuse the thieves. Back then they weren't covered and buried in sand you see,' his grandpa explained but then went a bit silent. 'Sad and ironic that centuries later, even if it is in the name of history and knowledge, the poor pharaohs still ended up losing their treasures eh,' he told Theo.

'Anyway, enough about dead people, tell me how school was today,' he asked, putting his book down. Theo shrugged his shoulders, 'Same old stuff, you know, learning, playing, listening to Hannah and Kacey be know it all's, and watching Simon get told off by the teacher for picking on some poor kid.'

'Hmm' Harold grumbled. 'That boy doesn't sound very nice or kind - Listen carefully Theo, you are a good one, I want you to stay like this and always remember if you can be anything, be kind,' Theo nodded, his grandpa always liked to remind him and Becki to be kind to everyone, he just hoped he wouldn't be expected to be kind to kids like Simon.

'Oh, look at the time, how is it so late already?' His dad James sprang up from where he was sitting, running around like the rabbit from the mad hatter's tea party, especially with his hair tied up in places like that. Harold and Theo looked at each other and Theo was unable to keep a straight face, the laugh bubbling up from his belly came out as a spluttering laugh.

Harold shared a conspiratorial smile with Theo, 'Would you like some help son?' he called out to James who had rushed into the kitchen, collecting a pot and pasta.

'No, no, it's all in hand, it's just boiling pasta, that's not hard,' James reassured.

Harold turned back to his book and turned the page, this page was full of pictures, 'Look at these Theo, they were found carved into stone in the Nile, they only discovered them recently due to the level of the Nile having reduced drastically,' he pointed to the images in the book.

Theo traced his finger over one of the images, it was a ripple, 'That there I believe was used for water or the 'N' sound, makes sense as it was found in the Nile. Oh, and look at this one, hang on let me look up what it is,' Harold said as he scanned to the bottom of the page for the explanation. It looked like a snake to Theo, sitting ready to attack. He didn't think it would mean anything friendly and happy. 'Ah this is the horned viper, and it can mean hidden dangers and divine punishment, hmm interesting.' Called it, Theo thought to himself, he had known just by looking at it that it wasn't a friendly or welcoming symbol, even though it was another language he guessed some things didn't need language, they just made sense.

Just then his mum, Phoebe, walked in through the door. She was drenched, he looked out the window, wow, it was pouring it down, Theo opened his mouth to ask her how her day was when the smoke alarm went off.

'What's your dad cooking?' she asked as she went to grab a flannel to wave at the smoke alarm to quiet it down, 'Pasta, just pasta, how does anyone burn pasta?' Harold asked, waving a towel at the smoke detector, 'not to worry, I have it all under control,' James shouted from the kitchen, but then they heard a loud crash. 'Change of plans, we're going out for dinner,' James announced sheepishly as he came rushing out of the kitchen.

At school the next day the gym was full of noise

as kids chatted while they waited for their lesson to start. Despite the doors being open the gym always smelt of stale sweat. Theo and Suhaan walked in side-by-side busy talking about their game the previous night.

'Man, that last round was brutal!' Suhaan told Theo, shaking his head as he spoke. Suhaan was usually moving around or shaking his head or gesturing with his hands as he spoke, it really didn't seem like he could ever be still.

Theo laughed. 'You totally saved me! If you hadn't covered that corner—'

A loud whistle cut through all the conversations. 'Alright, everyone! Time to split you up into two teams, as you may see if you cared to pay attention, it's dodgeball today', Ms. Brooke their PE teacher told them.

At the mention of Dodgeball, Theo's heart sank a little, it was his least favourite PE game, or was that the fitness test they did sometimes he wondered, his gaze fell on Simon who had a mean and excited look in his eyes, nope, nope, Theo was sure, he definitely hated Dodgeball the most. He turned to look at Suhaan and the boys shared a look of resigned misery, because Simon always took the game too far, hitting as hard as he could, and usually someone ended up in tears.

Theo glanced at Tamim, one of the smallest kids on their team, and the one who usually ended up in tears, nervously adjusting his glasses. 'You can stand kind of behind me, if you want, less chance of you getting hit,' Theo offered. Poor Tamim, for some reason Simon, Jack and Sarah always picked on him the most during Dodgeball.

'Thanks Theo, but today I'm going to go on the attack, better to go out fighting and take one of them out with me, well that's what my mum told me anyway,' he tried to smile confidently at Theo. 'Sounds like a good plan,' Theo reassured him, even though inside Theo didn't really believe that. You see Tamim was not very good at throwing the ball at anyone, but it was nice to see him be so brave.

Ms. Brooke blew her whistle again, this time to start the game. Balls flew through the air, some connecting and some miserably missing. Kacey and Hannah were gently throwing balls at each other; giggling as they missed. Theo rolled his eyes at them and turned away to find his own target. Aha! Amina was leaving herself open, target locked, weapon loaded, Theo rolled back his arm and released, (not too hard as his mum told him to always go a bit gentle with girls) and it was a direct hit! Amina turned around to glare at him, oh well, he looked around to see how Suhaan was doing, just then Suhaan got George, the two friends high fived each other and were having a mini celebration when they noticed Tamim. He was zipping around, not standing still, launching attacks while he ducked a rocket from Simon, narrowly avoiding a hit. Then Sarah's ball whizzed by his ear. Jack's throw missed by inches, bouncing off the wall. What was happening, was this really their Tamim?

Suhaan's eyes widened. 'Wow! Someone obviously had his Weetabix today,' he whispered to Theo, both of them dodging balls being thrown at them while also trying to watch Tamim in action.

Tamim kept dodging, darting left and right, the kids who were standing on the sidelines could see what was happening and they started cheering Tamim on. 'Go, Tamim, Go!' they shouted. Even Ms. Brooke smiled and shouted, 'Good dodge Tamim,' that was rare because she never complimented anyone.

Theo was catching his breath from dodging a shot from Lucy who had been running around trying to get him when he looked across at Simon to see him gather Sarah and Jack into a huddle, his face looked more angry than usual. They whispered, then looked at Tamim at the same time, this could not be good, Theo's spidey senses were going into overdrive, ok he didn't really have any special powers, but it was obvious something bad was about to happen

Theo nudged Suhaan. 'They're planning something.' At his words Suhaan looked over to catch them all looking pleased with themselves over whatever plan they had hatched, and it clearly was about Tamin because all three of them had their eyes glued on him like a target.

As the whistle signalled the start of the next round, Simon, Sarah, and Jack launched their balls in unison, a coordinated attack.

Tamim's eyes widened, he seemed to freeze, or maybe everything was going in slow motion, because it looked like Tamim was confused which way to run and that moment of hesitation cost him, because suddenly all at once the 3 balls connected hard, one on Tamim's head, another on his shoulder and a 3rd one right in his gut, whooshing the breathe out of him and making him fall to the floor with a thud.

Theo rushed over to help Tamim up, his eyes were a bit watery like he might cry, not that anyone could blame him, taking 3 hits in one go must hurt an awful lot. Ms. Brooke glared at Simon who merely shrugged his shoulders at her, trying to act innocent even though he was unable to hide his smirk. 'This is your first and last warning, play fair, no head shots, you know the rules' she told him in a stern voice.

There were not many kids left still in the game now, on Theo's side there was himself, Suhaan, Hannah, Josh, Ryan, and Jemma, while on the other side there was Simon, Jack, Sarah and Nyah. Ok, his team had the advantage, that was a good start. Suhaan came a bit closer and murmured, 'He's using Jack as a shield,' crouching next to Theo, pretending to tie his shoelaces. 'We need a plan.'

Theo nodded; eyes locked on their targets. 'We'll have to work together, we can't copy their plan, they would expect it. You take out Jack, that'll leave Simon open, and that's when I'll go in for the kill.'

Suhaan grinned. 'You got it.'

The boys were ready, the gym had gotten weirdly quiet, everyone was closely watching the players, hoping for Theo's team to win, but Simon was very good at this game. The whistle went, Theo watched Simon step further back behind Jack, Suhaan aimed right for Jack, and a split-second later Theo launched his own ball, just as Jack was pushed back by the force of the hit, the path had cleared enough for Theo's ball to whizz through and connect with a satisfying thud against Simon's chest.

'Out!' Ms. Brooke called, pointing at Simon and Jack. Theo and Suhaan high fived, but Simon wasn't done. His face flushed, he picked up a stray ball, Theo wasn't looking. In an instant, the ball rocketed through the air—smashing into Theo's face.

Everything went silent. The celebration turned to gasps as they watched Theo stagger back, hands clutching his nose as blood flowed between his fingers.

Simon grinned triumphantly. 'Shouldn't have

messed with me,' he muttered, loud enough for Theo to hear. Ms. Brooke was walking towards Theo to check on him, Suhaan took his chance then, without hesitation, he crossed the line, stomping toward Simon.

'Suhaan don't!' someone called. Too late, Suhaan shoved Simon hard, sending him sprawling to the floor.

The gym erupted into chaos—students shouting, Ms. Brooke's whistle was going crazy as a scuffle broke out between Suhaan and Simon. Ms. Brooke split the boys up, 'Right, Theo, you go to the nurse's office, and two will come with me to the head teacher, while the rest of you go and change, PE is done,' she shouted at everyone.

Chapter two

That evening, Theo was given the best seat in front of the TV by Becki, who usually hogged this seat, but getting a bloody nose during dodgeball seemed to make her feel very bad for him, as she also gave him total control of the TV by handing him the remote and declaring it a Theo night. As if that wasn't already more than enough, she then shocked him further by getting her favourite plushie, (it was a blue teddy thing that she carried everywhere), and telling him that bobo would look after him and make him feel better.

His mum, on the other hand, had not been handling this very well. She was cooking and every so often he could hear his mum say, 'We should change his school' and his dad for the hundredth time sighed and replied, 'Phoebs, people do not change their kids' school over a bad game of dodgeball, come on, be realistic please.'

While all this was happening, his grandpa came into the living room carrying a kitkat, he handed it to Theo and plonked himself down next to Theo.

'I think James has managed to calm down the mama bear in the kitchen, I thought she was about to go up to your school and huff and puff and blow the whole thing down,' he laughed at his own joke. 'Mums are great, and yours is one of the best, however maybe we shouldn't let her start the petition to ban dodgeball,' Harold told him. Secretly Theo thought maybe he wouldn't mind that so much, he got a bit hopeful, 'Do you think she would and could grandpa,' he asked, unable to hide the hope from his voice, the old man chuckled, 'Don't be silly, she won't really do that, she's just worried, and you're tougher than a little nosebleed. You come from a line of brave explorers, don't you forget that mate, now come on, let's go eat dinner, but promise me one thing, you won't tell your mother I gave you chocolate before dinner, she scares me,' he added only half-jokingly.

Dinner was full of the usual chatter around the table, Theo loved this bit of the day the best, when everyone came together and had a big update session. Becki usually liked to go first, telling everyone about who she played with, what she ate, who had a crush on who in her class.

His mum looked at him, 'Theo, would you like to go next love?' He shook his head no, he always liked to hear about the animal stories from his mum's vet clinic first.

The whole family paused to look at Phoebe to see if she had a story today, but she lowered her eyes to her plate and replied, 'Maybe I'll update after everyone has eaten,' immediately she was interrupted by everyone protesting, 'No mum, we don't get grossed out, please you have to tell us now,' Theo pleaded.

Taking a deep breathe, Phoebe began, 'So, it was a day like any other day, I had seen a few dogs and a cute little rabbit and then this cat was brought in,' she paused and took a sip of water, 'It was a cat named Whiskers, a lovely big Maine Coon, the owner thought she must have eaten something she shouldn't have, as she kept gagging, so I got Whiskers up on the table to take a look.'

Theo's imagination was running around in a spin, what could have been the gross part about this? 'Did you have to stick your hand in and get it, is that the gross part?' he asked.

'Erm, not quite, I was shining a light in his mouth when suddenly Whiskers coughed. It wasn't a little cough; it was a horrible, gagging, yucky cough which launched a hairball right into my face.' Everyone burst out laughing, 'Oh no mummy, you got yucky on your face,' Becki giggled. Theo could tell his mum wasn't done, 'Wait guys, there's more I think,' he told the others. 'Oh, you are so right, it got worse, you see the force of the cough must've triggered something, because at that exact moment there was a loud fart and a wet splat, there was cat poop on the wall, and it was slowly slithering down towards the floor'

Theo clutched his belly; his sides were hurting from laughing so much.

'Ok, enough about my day, now apart from the obvious,' she looked at Theo with a meaningful look, 'I am of course referring to the nosebleed, what else happened?' she asked. That's when his smile slipped.

Phoebe and Theo looked at each other, they had been doing this since Theo started school, and it was like his mum could almost read his mind and knew when Theo was about to say something his mum may not be too happy about. She sighed and closed her eyes for a brief second, like she was getting ready for bad news, 'It's not that bad, honest, so, erm, don't get annoyed at me, I forgot all about it and I had to be reissued my permission slip because I lost the original one. I have a trip, here's the trip permission letter,' he told his parents as he searched in his pocket and managed to come up with a scrunched-up piece of paper.

His mum rolled her eyes as she took the paper from his hand and looked at his dad, 'What? The Hawthorne men are a little absent minded, you knew this when you married me' he told her.

Phoebe tried to smooth out the paper and read out loud the important bits, 'A school trip, day after tomorrow, packed lunch needed, where is it, oh London History Museum, part of your history topic for this term, hmm sounds like it'll be a fun day out.'

Harold's ears seemed to perk up at that news, 'Ooo London History Museum, well that's marvellous, that's where all of your great grandpa's artifacts are kept, oh you were so small that time we went, how exciting for you to be going again,' he told Theo.

The way his grandpa's face had lit up, it seemed to Theo that Grandpa Harold was the most excited about his trip.

'It's just a bunch of old things grandpa, and we'll be mainly looking at the dinosaur displays I think,' he spoke through a mouthful of broccoli.

Grandpa Harold shook his head, his old man eyebrows creased up in a frown, 'A bunch of old things!' He spluttered, looking from James to Theo, then to Phoebe and Becki, then back at Theo, 'Nope, this won't do, eat up young man and then you and I have a date with history,' he declared, quickly chomping through the food on his plate, all the while muttering about history is the key to everything, and something about one day he'll be called a bunch of old things too. His grandpa sometimes went in hard with the dramatics, Theo had to work really hard not to roll his eyes at it all, even when he felt his dad trying to get his attention so that they could share a secret eye roll, the last time he gave in to his dad like this

his dad got them caught by starting to laugh, nope he would not look at anyone while he finished his dinner.

After dinner Harold and Theo went into the attic where they kept lots of old things they didn't really use. They had to make their way around a maze of boxes, precariously balanced on top of each other, full of old clothes that they intended to give to charity, old toys they had outgrown, old wires that might one day come in handy, just lots of old things. Amongst all of this was a pile that belonged to his grandfather, Harold pulled an old looking box off a bookcase, it had leather corners and was really dusty, making them both cough. Lifting the lid Theo leaned in, very curious about what would be in there, the first thing Harold took from the box was an old notebook, he handed it over to Theo.

'This,' Harold declared with some pride and sadness, 'belonged to your namesake, your great-grandfather Theodore. I've been waiting until you were old enough to show it to you, and it seems I just never got round to it, getting old is a nuisance let me tell you that, forgetting things and bones creaking,' he grumbled almost to himself. Harold then took out a small stack of photos that were tied with a ribbon.

'Here,' he told Theo, handing him the stack. Untying the ribbon, Theo looked through the pictures. In the first one stood a young man holding what looked like a shield, the man had a huge grin on his face. Despite the picture being so old and being in black and white, Theo could see that the shield had an animal face on it. 'Why does he look so pleased with that animal shield?' He wondered out loud, 'Hmm, let me see,' Harold said, leaning over Theo's shoulder and putting his glasses on to get a better look.

'Oh, that's not just any animal, that's a Jackal, they were usually linked to Anubis, he was god of mummification and afterlife.'

'Ok, but why does he look so happy with just that shield,' Theo still asked.

'It was his life's work I guess, It wasn't like the Tutankhamun, but it was still a significant find. From what I was told, my father had been obsessed with finding something out there in that desert. That shield is made of gold you know, you can't tell that in this photo, but it's in the museum, why don't you go take a look for yourself when you go. You can see all the other things he managed to find too.'

Theo blinked at the photograph, his fingers tracing the edges. 'I know you said before it was due to a sandstorm, but what exactly happened grandpa?' Theo asked.

'No one actually knows,' Harold admitted, setting the diaries on the table. 'What I do know is, he worked for months out there, visiting home every so often, then on one of these trips he found something leading him to believe he knew where to dig and lo and behold his gut proved right! He found all these artifacts; my grandfather Reginald was over the moon. But not everyone else, the locals believed he had disturbed a cursed place and didn't want anything to do with the items, so Theodore had them sent on with Reginald, for the London Museum. The plan, I believe, was for Theodore to follow on soon after, he was going to provide the information for each of the pieces, he stayed on to try and find out more information, but he never made it back.'

'There was an awful sandstorm that came with no warning, lasted for weeks. At the first signs of the sandstorm, the workers packed up, all running off saying the curse was coming to get them.

That's even what the officials tried to tell Reginald, that the curse was taking what it was owed. Ofcourse there's no such thing, it was just bad luck and too much obsession that got the better of Theodore.' Harold shook his head at his own words, he was not a very superstitious man, he tended to only believe in things he could see and understand, so people being scared because of superstitions didn't make sense to him.

'Wow, that must have been some sandstorm,' breathed Theo. He opened one of the diaries, revealing neat and tidy handwriting that described scorching days in the desert, the frustration of not finding anything for weeks, and just as they were ready to give up suddenly finding their way into a chamber full of jewellery, amulets weapons, gold coins and so much more.

Theo thought about how ancient people would have got buried with so much stuff, stuff they hoarded and treasured, only to then have other people come along and take it away.

'Grandpa, it doesn't feel right that the tombs just got broken into and all this stuff taken, even if we don't believe the same things they do, what if us taking this makes them unable to now have their afterlife?' his eyes reflected the concern that was clear in his voice and words. Harold paused in his rummage of looking through the box to look at his little grandson.

'Why Theo, that's very deep and very grown up of you. Yes, I can see why you would say that, I suppose maybe that's why so many people were terrified of things like curses and bad karma and stayed away. For better or worse, my father wasn't interested in the glory, I think he truly was interested in the history, and it has been so long, surely if they were going to move on, they would have already done so. I think the intention behind the removal of items is important, like if someone wanted to steal something as opposed to learn from it.' Theo slowly nodded his headed, he could sort of understand what his grandpa was saying, that Theodore was not trying to steal for the sake of greed, but he was trying to learn about what took place there, he was just trying to learn about history. 'I do feel bad for Theodore though, just when he found the tomb, he disappeared.'

Theo turned then to look at his grandpa, it made lots of dust mites start to fly, waving his hand trying to make them go away from his face, Theo stared intently at Harold, 'Grandpa, don't you think it's strange like even a little bit, that a sandstorm came and covered everything back up and that no one knows any information about the artifacts Theodore found. Doesn't it feel even a little bit like cursed or mysterious or something?' he demanded.

Harold looked at him like he had grown another head or something, then laughed, 'No, there's no such thing as curses, it was just bad luck, a sandstorm was passing through that way, Theodore didn't pay attention and paid the price, that's all.'

Theo frowned, deep in thought. 'Why didn't people just look for him at the dig site?'

Harold sat down on a pile of cushions, 'Well they did go back and look for him, my grandfather paid a lot of money to try and search for Theodore, but the sandstorm was brutal, the wind battered everything and covered everything back up, they couldn't find any sign of the tomb or Theodore.'

Theo found that really creepy, like a sandstorm covering up the tomb, and no one being able to find it or find Theodore, he wasn't convinced that it wasn't due to a curse, but he didn't say it out loud again, not when his grandfather clearly wouldn't believe it and might just laugh again.

Harold noticed Theo was very quiet suddenly, he got up and put his arm around Theo's shoulder's, 'Look Theo, history is mysterious, nature is mysterious, and while we can't say for sure exactly what did or didn't happen, as we weren't there, what we can be certain about is that there is usually a very good explanation for all the seemingly mysterious things that take place. Science and logic can explain everything.'

Theo was still thinking about Theodore and his mysterious disappearance the next day at school, while Suhaan was trying to talk to him. They sat on a square table that they shared with Hannah and Kacey.

'What did you get up to yesterday, I finished reading Alex Rider -'

'Quiet please' their teacher's voice cut over all the morning noise and talk, 'Settle down and let's get ready to do good listening and working today. Now I want you all to place your permission slips in the middle of your tables and Miss Maggie will come around to collect them all, no need for chatter while you do this,' their teacher Ms. Flanagan reminded them.

She was a small lady, barely taller than the kids, she had black hair and wore glasses. Every day at least once a day she would take off her glasses and press the bridge of her nose as if she was having a headache or trying not to say what she really was thinking, she mostly did that when George kept questioning her on everything.

They also had a teaching assistant called Miss Maggie, she was a bit taller, and she had big curly hair that seemed to be bigger than her head. She too had glasses, but hers were round like Harry Potter's.

Hannah and Kacey took out their permission slips and put them in the middle together, their slips were smooth and crisp. Theo pulled his slip out of his pocket, he tried to smooth it out a bit, Suhaan placed his slip on top, his mum always signed everything in funky bright pens, today she had used a glitter red.

'Who can remember what we discussed last week about our class book, Holes by Louis Sachar?' Ms. Flanagan asked everyone, there wasn't even a pause before Hannah and Kacey had their hands up, they were reaching so high it was like they would take off like rockets from their excitement in knowing the answers.

Theo watched Ms. Flanagan look around the room, no one else had their hand up, 'Ok then first Hannah then Kacey,' she told them.

Hannah smiled widely, 'We discussed themes, like friendship and loyalty, justice and Injustice-' she was clearly going to say more but Ms. Flanagan asked Kacey to start then, Hannah looked annoyed at being stopped.

'We also looked at writing devices like dual timelines, like using flashbacks,' she told the class triumphantly. 'Yes, thank you girls is there anyone else, oh Tamim, yes what would you like to add?' Theo looked over at where Tamim sat, he didn't usually answer class questions, so this was a surprise. 'You also told us about foreshadowing Miss, like something that hints at future events,' he spoke very quietly, Theo noticed he had been moved away from sitting next to Simon and Sarah, most likely cos of the incidents from PE the day before. Well, it had clearly been good for Tamim to move as he was finally talking in class to answer questions, maybe yesterday hadn't been all bad after all Theo thought to himself.

No sooner had he thought that when Simon and his cronies started up, even from across the room. Simon was making an ugly face and mimicking Tamim, 'blah, blah foreshadowing, blah' he was saying when their teacher narrowed her eyes at him. 'Quite enough of that Simon unless you want to spend your break and lunch indoors with me, doing extra work,' Ms. Flanagan warned. That was one good thing about Ms. Flanagan, she didn't allow anyone to get away with being mean, the warning worked, and Simon quickly closed his mouth and looked at the floor.

'Thank you Hannah, Kacey and Tamim for recapping for the class, now this morning I would like you to spend time doing creative writing, you are to imagine that you are Stanley and you will write a letter to your parents describing Camp Green Lake, you can quietly discuss with the person next to you to share ideas,' she told them.

No one in their class knew how to quietly share ideas, telling kids you can talk to the person next to you and then expecting quiet was just not going to work. Ever.

Turning to Suhaan, Theo started to speak, 'My

grandpa was showing me things from when his dad went on a dig in the old days.'

'Oh nice, so was he famous, did he dig up anything cool?' Theo shook his head, 'No, he only ever did one dig, he wasn't famous, he did go missing though on the dig, never to be found again. So, I guess that is pretty unusual, and the things he found are on display in a museum.'

'What, like abducted by aliens or magic or something?' Suhaan asked, more interested in the fact that Theodore had gone missing than that he had a display at a museum.

'No, my grandpa thinks he got lost in a sandstorm, but I think a curse must have gotten him, otherwise why can't he be found, right?'

'This is so awesome, like a real-life curse', Suhaan said in awe, truly impressed by the thought of a curse.

'Statistically speaking, most ancient tomb explorers got lost or ran into trouble because of poor maps or bad tools—not curses. It's way more likely your ancestor just had bad luck.' Hannah told them with a know-it-all tone.

'Yeh well, statistically speaking no one asked you so why don't you mind your own business,' he told her, not impressed with her butting in to make his story less interesting.

Hannah's nostrils flared and her shoulders rose and fell, he knew she was about to tell on him even before she opened her mouth.

'Ms. Flanagan, Theo and Suhaan are gossiping instead of doing their work,' she complained then pulled a smug face at Theo, smiling as Ms. Flanagan approached them frowning.

'Excuse me boys, if you can't do as you're told, I will be separating you, first and last warning,' she warned.

Hannah and Kacey grinned at each other, Theo ignored them and tried to concentrate on doing a better letter than Hannah, as the only way to get back at her here would be to be better than her. He tried to imagine what it would be like to be in a horrible camp surrounded by people he can't trust and got busy writing.

At lunchtime Theo and Suhaan sat at the long lunch table, their trays cluttered with half-eaten sandwiches and their favourite dessert, mini sugary donuts. The two were laughing and nudging each other as they tried to toss crumbs at a nearby seagull through the open cafeteria window. It was harmless fun—until Hannah appeared.

She planted her hands on her hips and glared at them. 'If you two can't eat like humans, then you don't deserve dessert,' she declared. Without waiting for a response, she reached over and snatched Theo's donut and headed to the bin.

'Hey! That's mine, give it back!' Theo snapped, standing up so quickly that his chair scraped loudly against the floor.

Hannah shrugged. 'You should've thought about that before playing with your food, clearly you didn't want it,' she dangled his donut over the bin.

Theo's eyes narrowed. He glanced at Suhaan, who was moving out of his chair looking ready to pounce and save the donut, Theo's eyes then landed on Hannah's tray, and her donuts……. Before he could think twice, he grabbed them, crammed them into his mouth in one quick motion, chewed dramatically, and spat the mangled remains back onto her tray.

Hannah froze mid-step, turned slowly, and stared at her ruined plate. Her face turned bright red, and then she screamed, stomping her foot.

'Fair's fair!' Theo said with a smirk, crossing his arms as Suhaan erupted into laughter beside him.

All the shouting had brought the dinner lady to their table, she quickly found out what had happened and took Hannah and Theo each by an elbow and marched them to the head teacher's office. He knew this meant big trouble, even as he walked closer to the office, the satisfaction of revenge was disappearing until it really didn't seem worth it anymore.

The school had called their parents to come in, Theo's Grandpa and Hannah's mum had arrived soon after the call, both looking annoyed as they walked into the head teacher's office and shut the door.

Hannah and Theo were sat outside the head teacher's office, only his secretary was there who kept looking over the top of her glasses at them with a stern look on her face.

'That was a mean thing you did,' Hannah hissed at him, immediately the secretary raised her head and turned to glare them at them both, 'Excuse me, there will be no talking while you wait.' Theo couldn't stop the smirk from spreading across his face, he quickly straightened his features as the door to the office started to open.

Mr. Ward, the headteacher, stood by the door. 'Right, in you both come,' he ordered them and then went to sit down at his desk again, waiting for Theo and Hannah to sit next to their grown-ups. Mr Ward leaned back in his chair, his hands steepled under his chin as he studied the two children. It was the dreaded stare, disappointment and annoyance all rolled into one which made kids want to hide under a table because they knew they had let Mr. Ward down.

'What happened today at lunch was completely unacceptable,' he paused to make sure they were listening. 'Disrespect, food fights, and shouting in the cafeteria—it reflects poorly on both of you and this school.'

Theo shifted in his chair, staring down at his shoes. Hannah tried to speak up, but Mr. Ward raised a hand, silencing her instantly.

'I was prepared to ban both of you from tomorrow's school trip,' he continued. 'Frankly, I don't think either of you deserve to go.'

Hannah's eyes widened in panic, and Theo felt a cold lump settle in his stomach. Missing the trip to the museum would be a real bummer because then they might be put into the other year 6 class and everyone would know they were being punished and laugh at them, not to mention their own class not letting them forget it.

'But' Mr. Ward said, his gaze softening slightly, 'your teacher, Ms. Flanagan, spoke on your behalf. She assured me that you are both usually well-behaved students and that this trip is vital for the material you'll be covering for the rest of the term.'

Theo let out a breath he hadn't realized he was holding.

'However,' Mr. Ward continued, his voice sharp again, 'this does not mean you're off the hook. After the trip, both of you will serve a week of after-school detention.'

'And you, Hannah,' Mr. Ward added, fixing her with a stern look, 'will also serve lunchtime detention for that week. Touching someone else's food was unacceptable behaviour.'

Hannah opened her mouth to protest, but the glare from Mr. Ward was enough to make her snap it shut again.

'Good,' he said briskly, leaning forward to rest his arms on the desk. 'I trust this will be the last time either of you causes this sort of disruption.'

'Yes, sir,' they mumbled at the same time.

As they left the office, he stole a glance at his grandpa to try and figure out how much trouble he might be in when he got home. Once they were in the car, he finally found the courage to ask, 'Am I going to be in a lot of trouble grandpa?' he asked nervously.

His grandpa gave him a very serious look, 'The way I see it, she touched your food for no reason, in my book that's a big no. What you did, well fair is fair, although you could have just eaten her donuts, what I'm confused about is why you chewed them and spat them back out? Waste of good food boy, we don't waste food.'

'I don't know either' Theo told him, his voice barely audible, he cleared his throat and continued, 'It was like for a minute there was no thinking, I just did it.' Harold sighed, 'Let this be a lesson, always take a moment and have a think about what you are doing, don't just rush in, okay?'

Theo nodded, he really was going to try and think before he acted next time.

Luckily for Theo, his grandpa downplayed the incident to his parents, calling it a kid's kerfuffle nothing more, 'it's all been dealt with now let it go,' he told James and Phoebe, he could tell his parents wanted to say more, but thankfully they did let it go. But not before they let him know how disappointed they were, that somehow felt worse than getting told off.

Chapter three

Egypt 1923

Theodore Hawthorne lay in his bed listening to the voices that were drifting up the stairs and all the way to his bedroom. He didn't mean to listen, but it was hard not to, the Inspector for Excavation Permissions, Mr Karim el-Sherif, and his assistant, Maurice Sinclair, were downstairs with his father, and Mr El-sherif was telling his father off.

They had been in Egypt for 6 months now, the discovery of the Tomb of Tutankhamun had made lots of people go almost crazy, well in Theodore's opinion anyway. Lots of people along with his dad and him, had all arrived in Egypt trying to find something wonderful for themselves.

Sometimes Theodore thought maybe everything that

could be found had already been found, because in the 6 months that they had been here their team had not found a single thing. He knew their permit had come to an end and they needed to pack up tomorrow, but that didn't explain the shouting.

Maybe Bahiti, his nanny, would know, she was sitting next to his bed knitting as she waited for him to fall asleep. 'Bahiti, why are the officials so mad, can't they just give father a new permit so we can stay longer?' he whispered to her.

Bahiti laid down her knitting needles in her lap and smiled kindly at Theo, 'Why don't we ignore the grown-up talk, let them sort it out, you just try to sleep, do you need the fan on, it is very warm despite the breeze coming in' she brushed his hair back gently.

Theodore sat up in his bed, 'I'm not a baby Bahiti, I'm big now, I do understand things you know' he told her indignantly.

Bahiti's low chuckle filled the room with a good vibe that made even Theodore's lips twitch, making him want to smile, but no, he wanted answers.

'Bahiti, if you know then please tell me, what's going on' he pleaded. She looked down at the little boy who had filled her life with happiness these last 6 months and

was due to be leaving in the next few days, she would miss him terribly, taking his little hand in her own she patted it, 'lie back down and I'll tell you what I know, but then you sleep, promise?' Thedore nodded happily and quickly snuggled down under the very light sheet and looked at her expectantly.

'Ok, so there are places in Egypt where digging is not permitted, for lots of reasons like it's too close to something dangerous, or its unstable ground or sometimes because people believe some areas are cursed, that nothing good will be found in those places, and your father, well, he has been naughty, and even though he knows the rules, he got some men to dig near the forbidden places.' She waited to see if he had understood everything, she had told him so far, Theodore looked deep in thought, 'Do you think there is treasure in those off limit areas Bahiti?' he asked finally.

Bahiti shook her head, 'Doesn't matter what might or might not be there Habibi, if it is believed that those areas are cursed then it is best people stay away, nothing good comes from looking in bad places,' she pulled the sheet up to his chin and laid a kiss on his head.

'Ok now sleep' she told him.

'Bahiti wait,' Theodore wasn't quite done yet, ' why are some places off limits and cursed, I thought curses are

like monsters and they don't really exist,' Bahiti bit her lip, oh she had opened a can of worms with this one she thought.

'Bad things only have power if people believe it, too many people have believed the curses in these areas, so it's just safer to stay away from them, why go looking for trouble eh? Now my nur e Ilahi, light of my life, close those eyes' she told him, when he opened his mouth, she quickly responded with 'nope, no more questions, now you sleep.'

The next morning Theodore got ready with a mission in mind, he was going to go and check out this cursed place for himself. He didn't believe in curses so he should be safe is what he told himself. As his father left for their dig site, Theodore jumped in the jeep, Reginald looked down at him in surprise. 'All these months you stayed away and today when we have to dismantle, you decide to join?' he asked. Theodore merely shrugged his shoulders, 'Last chance I guess' he told his father and stayed silent for the rest of the ride.

Their car drove past the permitted area onto where his father had started to dig illegally without permission, Theodore felt a weird flutter in his belly as they approached the people who were packing away tools and dismantling lights.

Theodore jumped out of the jeep and called out 'I'm just going to look around' as he ran off. 'Don't go far' Reginald called after him, but he was too late, Theodore had come with the intention of going as far as he could, to see if he could find anything himself. He ran past the workers, who were talking amongst themselves about what a relief it was to be done with digging here. Theodore stopped briefly when he spotted Faisal, the site manager.

Running up to Faisal 'Salam Alaikum Mr. Faisal, how are you today?' he asked, greeting the young man in his own language that Theodore had been trying to learn. Faisal greeted him with a big smile, 'Walaikum As Salam young Mr. Theodore, doing good, no complaints, and how are you doing this fine day?' he asked, even as he directed several men in how to pack things up properly. 'I know we are leaving today, and I know that my father got into a spot of trouble for digging this far out, I just wondered if you happened to know why everyone is so afraid of this place?'

'Ah Mr Theodore, so curious, children always ask so many questions, you want to know everything. Some places are just no good, you know bad. It's good we are leaving, come let's go' he told Theodore, just then one of the large flood lights fell to the ground with a loud clatter and everyone turned to look at where the noise was

coming from.

'What are you people doing, I said be careful when dismantling, here let me show you' Faisal walked off to help and Theodore used this distraction to run off further towards the place he thought was off limits.

Everyone was busy packing up, no one had the time to watch him or see where he was going.

Theodore walked for a long time, thinking there would be a sign or something to say when he got to the place that was meant to be cursed, like a danger sign or something, he looked around, all he could see was flat and empty desert, just more and more desert.

The sand was light and soft, swirling easily at his feet with each step, but somehow different—an odd, powdery texture, as if it hadn't been disturbed in ages.

Feeling defeated, tired, and very thirsty, Theodore came to a slow stop. His shoulders slumped as he realised it was all just made-up stories after all. He turned to go back, wait which way was back. Which way had he come from? The landscape was so flat, so repetitive, that every direction looked the same.

He turned one way, then the other, trying to catch sight of anything that might give him a clue on which way to go. The horrible realisation settled over him like a weight—he was lost, alone, and no one knew where he was. He felt tears burning at the back of his eyes, but he swallowed hard. No, he told himself. He would not cry. He must not cry. He would just pick a direction and keep walking. Eventually, he'd find someone or something to guide him back.

Theodore took a deep breath, the hot, dry air stinging his throat, and began walking, each step feeling heavier, as if the ground beneath him were tightening its grip with every passing moment, like he was slowly sinking in further into the sand with every step.

This was not good, he shouted for help, not knowing if anyone could hear him, he shouted as loud and long as he could, finally he saw some figures appear, oh he must have been closer to his father's dig site then he realised, he waved his arms around, shouting at them to hurry up, they were almost within reach of him, when suddenly, the sand engulfed him whole, out of sight.

Theodore quickly shut his mouth and eyes from fear that sand would go in, he felt like he was being pulled and tugged until he landed with a soft thud.

Luckily for him, the sand had not completely hidden where it had swallowed him but left a huge sinkhole. He was not aware that above him people were panicking and rushing, starting to dig, his father had been called, and he was promising rewards to anyone who would help. Below the people, away from all of that commotion, Theodore lay frozen, his body half-buried in cool, gritty sand, the darkness around him so complete it felt like a thick blanket. He couldn't see a thing—not even his own hand in front of his face. He could sort of hear people shouting his name.

Theodore stood up and tried to slowly move forward, but too scared to move from the spot. He felt the chill of the rough, stone walls against his fingertips. The air was heavy, almost buzzing with an eerie energy. It was like the whole place was holding its breath, waiting for something to happen. He swallowed hard, he turned his head to the left then to the right, but no, he couldn't see anything.

Where am I? he wondered, his heart pounding. Should he step forward and try to feel more of this wall, was it even a wall? What if there was a big monster waiting to eat his hand if he stretched it out any further? There were so many things going through his head, he felt the tears fall down his cheeks then, hot and salty dribbling down to his lips, he shouldn't have come, how on earth was he going to go back? Would he be stuck here forever, unable to get in touch with his family and be alone? He felt panic start to build inside his chest, making his lungs hurt, like something was squeezing his chest too tight. He felt like he couldn't breathe, just when he thought there would be no escape for him, a small light appeared above and a rope dangled down through the narrow opening, swaying gently like a lifeline from the outside world.

Theodore scrambled for the rope, his hands shaking as he gripped it and gave it a tug, shouting up, 'I've got the rope, please help me'. Slowly, he was pulled up, as he neared the top, he felt brave enough to look back, but the sand seemed to be closing in on itself, hiding its secrets again.

As the site workers pulled him out, the sand closed behind Theo, refusing to allow any further digging, like it had a life of its own. His father came rushing forward and checked him over briefly before ordering the workers to dig, 'Dammit people, there is something below us here, if you don't dig then I can do it by myself' he screamed as he reached for a shovel, but Faisal laid a hand on the shovel, stopping his father.

'Mr. Hawthorne, you know this area is off limits, we only did it one time to help the boy, the boy is returned, you are lucky, no more digging here.' Theodore watched Reginald and Faisal face off against each other, but whatever Reginald saw in the other man's eyes made him back down. 'Fine, finish packing up' he ordered and stormed off.

Theodore gave a hug of thanks to Faisal then ran after his father, constantly looking over his shoulder, there was something there and he intended to one day come back and find it.

Chapter four

It was trip day ! When they got to the school gate, the coach was already there, Theo felt as excited as everyone else looked. He let his dad give him a hug before he ran off to his classroom. They sat waiting to find out their trip buddy and group.

Theo was hoping not to be paired with Simon and his gang, no one liked being in a group with them, he kept his fingers crossed that he and Suhaan would be paired up together, he looked down to see Suhaan had his fingers crossed too, Suhaan looked up then and then motioned towards Simon and shook his head. Theo had to stifle a laugh that came out as a choke.

Ms. Flanagan read out the first group, 'Tamim, Ryan, Charlotte, Amina, Tyler and Farah. You are all with Miss Alison,' she then looked down at her book that she was reading from, Theo got a bad feeling in his belly, he felt like everything slowed down as she read out the next names, 'Simon, Sarah, Jack, Suhaan, Hannah and Theo will be in Miss Maggie's group.' He heard a sharp inhale of breath come from Hannah, for once they agreed on something, they did not want to be in this group. 'Ms Flanagan, this can't be right, I have to be in Kacey's group, please don't do this, we always pair up' Kacey pleaded along with Hannah, 'Ms Flanagan, this is not fair, we always work well together, we always do better than everyone else when we work together, please don't separate us.' she almost sounded on the verge of tears.

'Enough!' shouted Ms Flanagan, her eyes looked like angry, shiny glass marbles, 'No more debate, you are in the groups I have put you in and I will now pair you up myself, Hannah your trip buddy is Theo, Suhaan you are with Sarah and Simon and Jack you are together' she moved onto the next group, and ended by buddying up people as she wanted.

Kacey raised her hand, she looked almost tearful, 'Yes Kacey what is it now?'

'Please Miss, can we at least sit with who we want on the coach?' she asked. The whole class held their breath and looked at their teacher as they waited for the answer to that question, 30 pairs of silent pleas were directed at Ms. Flanagan.

Ms Flanagan bent her head, she took off her glasses and pinched the bridge of her nose for a few seconds before putting the glasses back on, she looked around at the whole class.

'Yes, you can sit next to who you want on the coach for the journey there, and if you behave then also on the journey back' she told them, happy little conversations erupted between everyone.

'Just please remember, your packed lunches are for lunchtime, not to snack on during the journey' she reminded them as she looked directly at Carson, he held up his hands 'whaat?' he said trying to look innocent, then he laughed 'My mums packed me extra this time so it doesn't matter anyhow,' Ms. Flanagan shared a look with Miss Maggie but didn't say anything, they ushered the kids out of the classroom and towards the coach.

Suhaan and Theo followed the kids out and onto the coach, Theo looked around, a lot of the seats were taken, he spotted the seat he wanted and the boys quickly got settled. Suhaan took the window seat as he liked it, which suited Theo as he liked to sit in the aisle seat.

Suhaan pulled out his book from his bag, it was a 'you choose: can you survive', where the reader has a choice of actions to pick from to try and get out of really hard situations, like the rainforest, which is where they were right now in the book.

They were not paying attention to the kids walking past them until they heard the voices of Hannah and Kacey, complaining from directly behind them about Simon and Jack, who were sat behind the girls, and were kicking and pushing the girls' seats.

'Oh great, I guess we're in for a really long journey' Theo muttered to Suhaan, 'Just tune them out, I do that when my little brothers are always fighting, watch' Suhaan looked at Theo and smiled even as Kacey was shouting at Simon, 'Just don't let it bother you' Suhaan said and turned the page of the book.

Theo tried, he really did try, but it felt impossible to block out the noise them lot were making. It was too hard to try and read like this, Theo leaned back in his seat instead and closed his eyes.

His mind wandered to Reginald Hawthorne, he must have loved and missed his son very much to have paid for a gallery to hold Theodore's artifacts. Harold had told him how the section that hosted the artifacts was dedicated to Theodore Hawthrone. How sad for Theodore to never know that his hard work was on display at an actual museum, it was probably more sad that he never got to spend time with his family and watch his son grow up. He suddenly felt something tickle his ear.

His eyes shot open, and he turned his head in time to catch Hannah leaning back into her own chair and giggling hysterically with Kacey.

'Yeh so funny, you don't like being bothered by Simon, but it doesn't stop you from bothering me, really mature Hannah, not' he told her, it worked like a treat in wiping the grin off her face.

Suhaan had stopped reading, 'what did she do to you?' he asked, as he had missed what she did, but still offended on Theo's behalf. 'She stuck something in my ear' he told his friend, giving his ear a wipe.

Suhaan got on his knees on his seat to look

over the top of the seat to narrow his eyes at Kacey and Hannah, 'not cool guys, carry on like this and you'll be as bad as them' he said nodding his head towards Simon and Jack.

Hannah pouted and crossed her arms over her chest in a huff, 'I was only joking with him to wake him up and stop him snoring' she replied huffily.

'Oi that's a lie!' shouted Theo and he copied Suhaan's pose to look behind him, 'I wasn't even asleep, you were just being mean, how can I snore if I wasn't even asleep' he was almost shouting in his indignation now. Miss Maggie heard the arguing and got out of her seat to come towards them, she looked like she was surfing as she tried to keep her balance, 'Ok kids, ok, let's all calm down, boys please sit down properly and girls, remember personal space please and respect' she told them.

Kacey's face dropped open in a big 'o', and her eyebrows shot up, 'I wasn't even doing anything' she complained, 'Stop, I don't want to hear another peep out of any of you or else I will leave you all at the reception of the museum' Ms. Flanagan spoke from behind Miss Maggie, they hadn't seen her coming up behind as she was much shorter. The four of them quickly quietened down and tried not to make eye contact with Ms. Flanagan. The rest of the journey was quite uneventful after that, he even got to read the book with Suhaan, it was fun even if they did get caught by a boa constrictor and didn't make it out of the jungle this time, they knew which route to avoid for the journey home.

After what felt like ages, but according to his watch was like 2 hours, the coach pulled into the parking lot of the museum.

Everyone always made a big deal about visiting London, but it didn't look that wow to him. The clouds were still looking like they were unhappy, the rain drizzled the same, everything looked a bit grey here like it did in Odinbury, the only difference right now was the great big buildings that were everywhere.

It was like there was a Bermuda triangle of museums here, right in front of them there was a very large building, with huge windows, and down one side of the building there were lots of flags blowing in the wind which announced that this was London History Museum. Across from this was another very old looking building, the bricks looked grey, it was slightly smaller but it also had

those large standing flags and this one said London
Science Museum, and finally the 3rd one which
finished off the weird triangle was a building
slightly smaller than the science one, this one
didn't have any flags like the other two, it did have
very intricate writing carved into the front in large
letters which let everyone know it was an art
museum.

Theo would have liked to have visited the
science museum instead of the history museum,
but now that he knew it was here, he was thinking
he might ask his mum and dad if they could come
and visit it themselves one day. Suhaan noticed
him looking at the building and paused himself, 'I
heard it has really cool things, like a space section
with real rockets, I wish we were going there
instead' he said out loud wistfully.

Kacey sniffed at that and turned around so
sharply her hair which was in a plait flew through
the air to come and coil around her neck like a
snake, it freaked Theo out a bit.

'Of course you would only pick one museum to
visit, I wish we had the time to visit all three and
complete the trifecta' she told them haughtily,
Suhaan mouthed 'What's a trifecta?' Theo

shrugged his shoulders but then thought it might mean something to do with all 3. Well why couldn't she just say that?

'Why do you always have to be so extra Kacey? Why can't you just say all three like a normal person?'

'There's nothing wrong in knowing different ways and better ways to say something,' Kacey told them, turned really fast making her hair do that weird flip and coil thing again and walked off in a huff.

The whole class, including their teachers, shuffled into the museum slowly, the kids looked around them and many gasped in surprise to see hanging above them was a huge skeleton of a whale. 'How did they get it to hang up there?' Sarah asked, tilting her head all the way back to see the full effect of the whale. 'Do you think it will fall down on us?' asked Amina.

'Look at how many of us could have fit inside its belly at the same time' breathed Kacey. The children spent several minutes, craning their necks and just enjoying looking at the remains of the Blue Whale.

'You can all learn more about sea creatures in the Marine Invertebrates Gallery. Now please remind yourself of the rules of when we are on a trip. If you wonder away from your buddy, you will automatically get an 'F' for your history assignment which, will be centred around the museum visit'

Ms. Flanagan looked at George who had his hand up, 'George before you ask, when you need the toilet, I expect your buddy to wait outside and other than toilet break you are to remain within an arm's reach if not shoulder to shoulder with your assigned buddy.'

George looked deflated as his joke had been ruined.

Miss Maggie collected her map and bag with worksheets and pencils and ushered her group towards The Fossils and Dinosaurs section, the other groups had different starting points so they could all avoid each other to create less congestion, they were going to meet up at lunchtime in the lunch hall and then separate again until it was time to head home.

As they walked towards the fossils section they started to drift into two groups of 3 kids, Theo,

Suhaan and Hannah in one line and Simon, Jack and Sarah in the other. Miss Maggie considered telling them to get into their two's but then thought they seemed happy and were not making any trouble, so she let them continue.

George could be heard from behind them start to complain about why they couldn't start from the dinosaur exhibit, that it was the best bit of the museum.

'You will get your turn George, now buddy up and start walking please' Ms. Flanagan told him as the groups walked away from each other.

Miss Maggie made them all pause for a minute as she handed them all their worksheets, Theo quickly scrolled through the questions to see what they had to do.

Hannah was doing the same thing, they both had their heads down as they entered the dimly lit room and were startled by a huge dinosaur that seemed to lunge right at them, even Simon and Jack got startled and gave a nervous laugh to cover their scare.

'It's huge, it must be a T-rex' exclaimed Jack, 'No Jack, look at the long neck and tail, that's a diplodocus or a brachiosaurus' Hannah told him. Jack ran over to read the information sheet next to the dinosaur, Theo didn't bother. As much as he hated to admit it, Hannah was usually right about these things.

The group wandered through the towering halls of the rest of the exhibit, their voices echoed faintly as they stopped at each massive window display. Behind the glass, skeletons of ancient giants loomed—Tyrannosaurs with jaws gaping wide, long-necked sauropods caught mid-stride, and even a raptor frozen mid-pounce. The air buzzed with their excitement.

Theo pressed his nose against the glass, staring at a perfectly preserved dinosaur feather trapped in amber. "Can you imagine?" he whispered to Suhaan, 'This thing is millions of years old. What if it still has dino DNA in it?'

Suhaan adjusted his glasses. 'Maybe it does, but I'd rather not meet a cloned velociraptor, thanks. I've seen *Jurassic Park.*'

Further along, Simon, Jack and Sarah, were busy finding new ways to cause mischief. Simon had somehow picked up a claw replica from an open display table and was using it to sneak up on Miss Maggie, 'Rawr!' he growled, making her jump and yelp at the same time.

Miss Maggie had also dropped her notebook when he scared her, picking her things up she looked at Simon in annoyance, 'Simon! That's not funny!'

"It was to me!" Simon laughed, tossing the claw to Jack, who fumbled and let it bounce onto the floor. Sarah seemed to be annoyed with this too, which was unusual as she usually went along with everything they did, 'guys be more careful'.

'Oh chill out Sarah, these are all fake' he walked off but Miss Maggie marched up to him and whisper shouted at Simon, 'What were you told about behaving in the museum?'

Simon flashed her his most innocent grin, 'To have fun and enjoy the exhibits?'

Miss Maggie raised an eyebrow, 'Simon Underwood, you will stop messing about this instant, if you can't do that then I can leave you at the reception for the rest of the trip' she warned.

Simon's grin vanished, 'I, er, I won't do that again Miss,' he told her looking like he actually meant it for a change.

As the group moved to the next exhibit, Theo noticed a gigantic claw suspended in a case, labelled **'Therizinosaurus Claw – Replica.'** Miss Maggie handed out sketchpads and instructed everyone to draw it. Theo started sketching the curve of the claw, but his attention kept going to Hannah, who was dramatically shading hers like she was competing for a prize.

'Hey, Theo,' Suhaan whispered, pointing to his own sketch, 'Do you think it looks more like a claw or… a banana?'

Theo squinted, 'Maybe a claw that might eat bananas?' Theo answered and they started laughing, Suhaan was terrible at drawing, and he didn't mind admitting it.

Hannah overheard and shot them both a withering look, 'At least mine doesn't look like someone's shopping list,' Theo rolled his eyes, Hannah and Kacey were always so competitive, sometimes he wondered how they managed to stay friends let alone be best friends.

By the time Miss Maggie called for everyone to finish, Simon had drawn a claw with laser beams shooting out of it, and Sarah had filled her page with doodles of hearts and stars. Miss Maggie inspected their work, sighed, and reminded everyone that the exhibit was about dinosaurs, not comic books or stationary design.

The group was full of laughter as they filed out of the exhibit, heading toward the next display. Theo couldn't help but glance back at the towering skeletons one last time, a small shiver running down his spine. Dinosaurs may have been extinct, but they sure knew how to leave an impression.

Miss Maggie was enjoying herself more than she had expected to, smiling she, led them toward the next exhibit. 'Alright, explorers, time to journey forward in time. We're leaving the age of dinosaurs and stepping into human history.'

They entered a huge room titled 'Ancient Civilizations Through Time.' The room stretched out like a timeline, each section giving you information on a different chunk of time.

The group followed Miss Maggie towards the first display, behind a glass wall on a huge table was something that looked like a square pyramid, 'Who knows what this is?' she asked them all, the silence was quite telling that none of them knew, not even Hannah. It was Suhaan that spoke up, 'Miss, it looks like a pyramid gone wrong' he told her hesitantly. Miss Maggie nodded, 'Good try, it's a replica of the Ziggurat of Ur, a ziggurat is an ancient Mesopotamian temple. It was also the world's first skyscraper of its time' she told them, looking at them waiting for them to be impressed. Simon scoffed, 'It doesn't look like it could have been that tall Miss,' he told her and moved on to the next display. Miss Maggie called Simon back and continued, 'Listen, we aren't done here, so Mesopotamia's innovations included cities, writing and organised agriculture, and without these inventions the next civilisation we are going to look at, the ancient Egyptians, would not have flourished as they did' she told them.

'Did Mesopotamian's have mummies too?' Hannah asked, she had moved on a bit to stand next to Simon and look at the Ancient Egyptian display. As the rest of the group moved over to look at the mummies, Miss Maggie followed, reading from her notes, and the wall display. 'I think that is just specific to the ancient Egyptian culture Hannah, which is what we are looking at now. Ok so here you'll see how the ancient Egyptians honoured their Pharaohs and prepared them for the afterlife. This,' she gestured to the mummy, 'is an example of how they preserved bodies through mummification.'

'What, no way, is that a real actual mummy in there?' Suhaan asked.

'Oh no, Suhaan, this one is a replica. But it's an exact copy of a mummy that was found many years ago.'

'It feels kind of weird for us to be looking at someone who is supposed to be dead, don't you think?' Hannah asked, looking at the mummy, unable to take her eyes off it. 'Look Hannah's found her twin' Simon sniggered, but Jack looked a bit confused. 'How is that her twin? I don't get it' he was mumbling.

Miss Maggie ignored them to answer, 'I guess that's true, but we should also think about how studying these artifacts teaches us so much about their lives, beliefs, and even their diets!'

They walked along to a glass display which held ink pots, brushes, scrolls and papyrus. The papyrus had hieroglyphs.

'Does anyone know what these are?' she asked pointing to the hieroglyphs. Theo was quick to answer, 'Those are hieroglyphs Miss, the Egyptian alphabet,' he told her and felt pleased with himself at her approving look.

'Well done, you seem to know quite a bit about this, very impressive,' Simon pulled a face at him, 'Very impressive' he mimicked.

'Looks a bit like emoji's Miss, so the ancient Egyptians were using emoji's before we even had internet!' Jack laughed at his own joke; Theo laughed because that's exactly what he had said to his grandpa.

Simon pointed to a symbol, 'Hey, that one looks like a bird! 'Miss Maggie nodded, 'That's right Simon, that's the vulture, which stood for the letter 'A' or the word 'great.'

'What about this one Miss Maggie, it looks like a dog/wolf,' Jack asked. Theo looked at the symbol, he knew this one from his grandpa, 'That's a jackal, it's to do with death, or guardian, sometimes they can have different meanings' he told them. Miss Maggie looked like she would burst with happiness at someone knowing all this, 'That's right Theo, well done.'

The group continued to look at different symbols, making little notes on their worksheets, trying to figure out what the messages might mean. Before long Miss Maggie called out, 'Come on, everyone! We need to go meet the others for lunch.'

They hurried out of the exhibit room and were following the signs for the lunch hall. On their way they passed a closed exhibit, a thick velvet rope stretched across the entrance, there was also a sign which read, 'Do Not Enter Closed for Restoration.'

Theo squinted into the darkness beyond the

rope, it just looked like a boring collection of things on display. Standing there, the hairs on Theo's arms prickled, as if the room was watching him— waiting for something, or someone.

As a shiver ran through him, he looked up at the sign, it read Hawthorne gallery of antiquities, oh! This was it! His great grandpa's section. Theo had almost forgotten all about this.

Hannah bumped into him as he had stopped walking, 'What are you looking at?' she asked and looked up, she looked at the name and then him and then the name again, but she didn't say anything. She hurried passed as she knew Kacey would be saving her a seat or if she was first, she needed to save Kacey a seat.

Theo looked back into the room, it was as if a whisper was reaching out from the room and coming towards him, trying to curl around him. Theo shook off the feeling and followed everyone to lunch.

Chapter five

Suhaan waited until they were sitting down and were eating before he spoke up, 'I noticed that last gallery we passed had the same surname as you, you looked kind of spooked, you know you can talk to me right,' he told Theo as he munched on his sandwich.

Theo looked around at everyone, the others were busy eating and talking, comparing their stories from the different exhibits, he just didn't want anyone to overhear, 'You know I was telling you about my great grandpa, well that exhibit holds the things he found' Theo told him, with a shrug of his shoulders, as if it wasn't a big deal.

Suhaan's eyebrows shot up, 'oh, wow, you do realise that is so cool that your family owns part of the museum' he spoke excitedly. Theo shook his head, 'No, no, that is so far from the truth, they donated the artifacts they found, and they donated money to name the exhibit after my great grandpa' he corrected his friend. Suhaan shrugged his shoulders, 'tomahto, tomato, still means you have a share in the museum. Couldn't you have picked something more fun to have a share of?'

Theo looked at Suhaan, 'Mate it wasn't me who picked was it? It was my great, great grandpa, like well before I was born you know.'

'Shame, but still cool' Suhaan told him as he scrunched up the foil his sandwich had been in. He went over to the bin to throw it away and was coming back to their bench when Simon suddenly stuck out his feet to make Suhaan trip over.

Suhaan fell to the ground with a groan, Theo ran over to help him back up, Simon, Sarah and Jack were all pointing and laughing at Suhaan.

'Suhaan looks like you should get new glasses, these ones clearly aren't working' sniggered Simon. Theo looked over his shoulder giving him a glare, 'Looks like you have ape feet more like' he snapped at Simon, as he helped Suhaan up.

From the worried look on Suhaan's face, Theo

had a bad feeling that Simon was coming towards him. 'He's behind me, isn't he?' he asked. Suhaan nodded slowly before shouting duck and pushing Theo out of the way of Simon's fist that was coming right at Theo.

Unfortunately for Simon, Theo ducked and moved right into Simon's midsection, which sent Simon sprawling onto the floor. Now the kids who were closest to them were laughing at Simon.

'Aw, what's the matter? Didn't watch where you were going?' Theo called out, laughing loudly.

Simon's face turned bright red. He glared at Theo, his eyes narrowing into sharp slits.

As Simon pushed himself off the floor, Theo stopped grinning. He could tell this was about to go south. Slowly, he began backing away.

Simon jumped up quickly, his expression angry and lunged toward Theo.

'Oh no,' Theo muttered before spinning on his heels and sprinting back toward the galleries they'd already visited.

The commotion caught Miss Maggie's attention. Before Ms. Flanagan could figure out what was going on, Miss Maggie clapped her hands and called out brightly, 'Time to move on, team!' She herded the rest of her group towards the way Simon and Theo had gone with a big, panicky smile, pretending everything was perfectly under control.

Hannah looked annoyed at cutting her lunch short and picked up her bag to hurry after them, 'why are you in such a rush?' Kacey asked her.

'He's my trip buddy, I have to catch up and be at an arm's length remember,' she told Kacey as she ran past Suhaan who had started running after Simon, with Miss Maggie Jack, and Sarah rushing after Hannah now.

Theo's heart was thumping as he ran without thinking, he ran past the Hawthorn Gallery, but something made him pause and run back and then jump over the rope that was meant to keep people out.

The lights were dim in here, like the museum was trying to save money, there were lots of displays with sheets over them, Theo scanned the room for a good hiding place, there was a tall glass display, the sheet had fallen off. Theo ran to the vitrine and covered it back up with the sheet then crouched down behind the wooden bottom half. He tried to breathe slower and through his mouth, so as to be as quiet as possible and not give away his location.

From his hiding place he could see the entrance if he peeped his head out a bit, he quickly brought his head back in, because just then Simon had entered the gallery, Simon had been close enough to see Theo enter.

'I know you're in here you dorkasaurus, who else would run into a gallery instead of going to a teacher' Simon called out, ah damn, thought Theo, he should have just gone to a teacher, how could Simon be thinking more clearly than him?

'There's no grown-ups here, I'm gonna find youuuuuu' Simon said on a sing song, just as Suhaan and Hannah ran into the Gallery. Suhaan was out of breath, and Hannah managed to knock into an open display table. Suhaan bent over resting his hands on his knees for support while he tried to talk, 'too late….' he panted, 'Miss Maggie on the way…. Leave Theo alone.' He stood upright and leaned against a pillar which had a golden shield with a jackal face on the front, his elbow accidentally knocked into the shield.

Hannah and Suhaan watched in horror as it crashed to the floor with a great big clang and clatter, but the metal it was made from must have been very strong as it didn't dent, instead it rolled on its side towards Theo and then clattered to a stop. All eyes went to the spot it had stopped at, and they spotted Theo's shadow. Simon smirked and strode towards Theo, Miss Maggie skidded into the gallery then, 'boys, enough, you will all stop messing around and head back with me now' she said in a stern voice.

Jack and Sarah came running in and bumped into Miss Maggie making her fall over, Simon used this chance to rush towards Theo with his fist raised and brought it crashing down towards Theo's face, Theo had managed to reach the shield and brought it up to protect himself, which meant Simon's fist connect with the shield and he howled out in pain.

Miss Maggie got up off the floor and dusted herself off, then came towards Simon, 'Enough!' she shouted as she inspected his hand.

Theo's eyes though were drawn to the shield, it was vibrating, he could hear the hum, and it was getting louder. As he kept looking at the shield he realised there was a light spinning around the rim of the shield, at first he thought it was the light playing tricks, Suhaan came to stand next to him 'Hey look, why is it doing that?' Suhaan asked.

Hannah came forward to take a look too, 'That's strange, look Miss Maggie, look, the shield looks alive, oh my goodness, look its swirling, its rising,' she exclaimed almost hysterical now. By the time Miss Maggie and the others looked over, the swirling light was gathering speed and height like a tornado. It was gathering dust as it spun faster and faster, strangely the furniture and objects remained untouched, what was being affected were all the people. One by one they were being lifted off the floor, the spinning light and sand and wind was making it impossible for them to see what was happening, all Theo could feel was being lifted off his feet, his toes scraping the floor, he scrambled to try and grab at something, anything, he managed to grab onto the top of the glass display, but his fingers were slowly slipping until he was fully caught up in the tornado with the others.

The tornado spun faster, the hum growing louder, as the dust thickened, blurring their vision. Suddenly, with one last flicker, the lights went out completely, plunging the room into darkness. And just like that—complete silence.

When the lights flickered back on, the gallery was empty. Every trace of the kids and Miss Maggie had vanished, leaving only a thin layer of dust settling quietly on the floor.

Gary, a new museum attendant, thought he heard some noise coming from the closed off exhibit, he came to the entrance listening, but he couldn't hear anything else. Cautiously he stepped over the rope and entered the room, he turned the lights off and then on again trying to see if that stopped the flickering, ah that did the trick, nope it didn't the light started flickering again. Oh well, it was a closed off exhibit, he would get that looked into later he thought, not like anyone was going to come in here anyway.

Chapter six

Egypt

Theodore stood in the dimly lit back room of the Cairo Museum, he almost felt sick with excitement and nervousness. For years he had been going back and forth between his home in the UK and his work in Egypt, all the while trying to find out more about that tomb he had fallen into as a child. But the people here did not want to talk about that area, they refused to admit there was even a tomb there. So far, he had learnt through his research that there may have been a powerful man who was buried there, but he had not come across anything solid, until now.

Just this morning a crate had arrived for him; he had paid a huge amount of money for this. It was found within the artifacts taken from the Temple of the veiled ones who served Ma'at, the Egyptian goddess of order and balance.

His friend Ahmet had heard that there was a scroll that had been found, and poor Ahmet had raced over to try and get his hands on this before anyone else, as he knew Theodore had been working for so long on trying to find information on a secret tomb. He owed Ahmet hugely for this.

Theodore approached the crate, there was a note on top, he picked it up to read it.

Theodore my friend, I have done as you asked, but even though I know you will ignore my request, I implore you, when you read the scroll inside, let that be enough for you. Don't go chasing things that are meant to stay buried – much love Ahmet. PS I was almost bitten by a snake just opening this crate, and before you ask, no I shall not be joining you on your madness

Theodore laughed and opened the crate, out popped a snake, 'argh' he gasped and then realised it was a toy snake with another note attached to its body 'at least your snake was just a toy – A' he shook his head at Ahmet's humour. Inside, wrapped in layers of linen, was the scroll. The fragile papyrus was cocooned in protective cloth, its edges browned with age. His hands trembled slightly as he reached in, lifting it with special gloved hands.

'Could it really be...?' he whispered, his voice barely audible in the room.

Theodore placed it gently on the table, unwrapping the linen with slow, deliberate care. The scroll's surface was covered in intricate hieroglyphs, faded but still visible. Symbols of power, protection, and something more— warnings. His heart hammered in his chest.

His eyes scanned over the scroll;

Tonight a very dark deed was done, we the priests of Ma'at managed to rid the world of the traitor, Pharaoh Nakht-Ankh. Many years ago, our beloved Pharaoh Amunotep was betrayed by his most trusted advisor, Nakht-Ankh. In his greed for the throne, he killed Amunotep and declared himself Pharaoh.

He was cruel to the people, he was greedy, laying his hands on all the gold he could. Amunotep's loyal guards came to us with a plan to overthrow him.

For his crimes, Nakht-Ankh was sentenced to death. We cursed his tomb, trapping his spirit and that of anyone else who entered with greed in their heart.

There is no name for this tomb, only a warning: 'Stay away from this place. Those who enter will share in the cursed one's fate, forever guarding the treasures they seek.'

Theodore's heart thumped, he felt a mixture of happiness, excitement and something else he couldn't describe. Was it a bit of fear? No, surely not, just excitement he told himself. He didn't believe in curses, but finally, he had found what he had been looking for, proof and validation that something was down there. He couldn't wait to get out there and start looking, he had been creating maps of possible areas for a long time and thought he had narrowed it down, but now with the confirmation, he felt a renewed sense of purpose. Thankfully there were no more bans around the area he wanted to dig in, as the new government wasn't as superstitious. Which was why he didn't want the scroll getting into anyone's hands, he didn't want anyone else getting to this tomb before him.

His heart still hammering he sat down to write 2 letters, one to his wife, apologising that he would be delayed but he was very close now and soon would be home for good. The second letter was to his father, Reginald, who had been hunting for a find for his whole life, it was only right that he be here for the dig that Theodore was about to start.

Chapter seven

Theo blinked, his eyelids heavy and gritty, he rubbed his eyes and then opened them in shock and surprise, they didn't just feel gritty, there was sand on his face and hands. He sat up, this was not his bedroom. This was not any room he had ever seen before. The air was warm, thick, and smelled really old and earthy. A faint light illuminated the walls, not from any torch or lamp, but from the shimmering of, was that hieroglyphs on the walls? They glowed, and he wasn't sure, but it seemed like they hummed, like a vibration coming off of them, they were also casting a pale, golden light into the room. Did he fall asleep at the museum? But wait, the exhibit room wasn't this cold, or smelly and it didn't have glowy hieroglyphs on the walls.

'Where... am I?' he muttered, his voice echoing off the walls.

A groan sounded nearby. Suhaan was stirring, rubbing his eyes. 'Theo?' His voice was hoarse. 'What's going on? Did we... fall asleep on the trip?'

'Trip? No, I—' Theo stopped. He tried to piece it together. They'd been in the museum, right? Then a sandstorm started and now they were not in the museum, this really couldn't be the museum, could it?

Around them, Simon, Sarah, Hannah, Jack and Miss Maggie were starting to make noises, like they were waking from a sleep too. 'Guys... this isn't funny. Where are the lights?' Sarah asked, her anxiety very clear in her voice.

Miss Maggie looked around her like a meerkat, left, right, then left again, 'Everyone, stay calm', she instructed them, her voice sounding a bit too high. Theo didn't think it was the right time to point out that she herself didn't sound calm. 'Is anyone hurt?' she asked, her voice a bit wobbly.

A chorus of 'No' and 'I don't think so' echoed back.

They all slowly got to their feet, one by one, brushing sand off their clothes. Jack stepped towards the wall next to him, his hand touching the cold stone, he shivered at the touch. 'Oh, I don't know why I thought this was going to be warm, it sounded like it was making a noise' he whispered, Theo went up to Jack, 'I know right, like its humming or something' he reached out to touch the wall too, it was very cold, he quickly pulled his hand away again.

'I think it's just a room in the museum, nothing to be afraid of' Miss Maggie tried to convince Jack, and them all.

'It might be a really bad underground part of the museum; you know how the dinosaur was interactive' Simon suggested. Hannah looked at him for a moment, 'You know that might be the only explanation that makes sense, we must have fallen into a different part of the museum, we just need to find our way back out.'

Theo looked around, his eyes caught sight of the shield that had started the problem, he grabbed it up and put his arms through the straps to wear it on his back like a backpack. 'Hey, why do you get to have the shield, what if one of us wants it?'

Simon complained. 'Well considering we were in the Hawthorne gallery, his great grandpa's gallery, and considering his great grandpa found this in Egypt, I would say it makes sense, duh,' Suhaan retorted back.

Miss Maggie looked at Theo, 'Is that true Theo, was that exhibit your family's?' she asked him, all the kids looked at him then, he felt a bit embarrassed with everyone looking at him. 'Er yes, it was my great grandpa Theodore Hawthorne, he went missing in Egypt, but he found everything in that room, this shield included, on a dig, before he went missing' Theo explained.

'That's all very nice and everything, but why are those hieroglyphs glowing?' Sarah asked no one in particular. 'It must be part of the feel of the room, you know like an escape room, look it has only one exit, let's just follow it, it must lead us out to the main museum again,' Hannah decided and headed for the little doorway that looked like it had been carved into the wall.

'Wait Hannah, before we rush to do that, we should take a moment and think, have a look in this room properly maybe' Theo suggested, his grandpa's words coming back to him to think before acting, and this felt like one of those times where thinking was very important.

'Theo, there is only one obvious doorway, let's go and take a look, come on,' Miss Maggie suggested as she followed Simon and Hannah out of the room. They all filed out of the room, in a single file, Theo was last to leave, as he walked past the glowing hieroglyphs, he reached out to touch them again, to see how they were glowing but he couldn't see any way to explain it. He was getting a funny feeling in his stomach, he didn't like the feeling and couldn't fully explain it, he just knew something wasn't quite right.

The passage was dark and narrow, and the top was very close to their heads, if he stretched his hands out, he could feel the cold rough walls with his elbows still bent, that's how narrow it was, clearly not meant to be a nice and leisurely experience. The air grew noticeably colder, and the walls seemed to press in closer with every step. Rough stone scraped against their shoulders, and the faint echo of their shuffling feet added to the weird feeling. Theo wished they had a torch or something… 'Miss Maggie, do you have your phone on you, it has a torch doesn't it?'

He heard her shuffling around and then finally the passage lit up from the small light, ok, this was a bit better or was it. Now he could see the walls, they didn't look like it was meant for a class trip, he even saw some little bug scuttle across the wall.

Hannah who was at the front of their line turned around to speak to the rest of the group, 'Guys, I think there's some light up ahead at the end, come on we must be close to the exit,' she sounded excited, she also sped up a bit.

Theo couldn't see much, due to being right at the end, but he sped up too. The floor was a bit uneven, like it wasn't built very well, but they continued, well there was no other way to go. Simon grumbled behind her about the tight space, and not having finished his lunch, feeling hungry.

Then, suddenly, Hannah stopped dead in her tracks. Simon who was right behind her bumped into her, nearly toppling both of them. 'Oi, what's the big idea?' he snapped.

Miss Maggie who was walking slower managed to stop without bumping into them, she held a hand out behind her to stop the rest of them. 'What's going on, why have we stopped?' Theo called out from the back.

'Guys...' Hannah's voice wavered, 'I don't think we're in the museum anymore.'

Jack turned around to Suhaan and Theo, while Sarah clutched at Miss Maggie's arm, 'She doesn't think we're in the museum anymore' he repeated for them.

Everyone who was behind Hannah started murmuring about what she meant, well where are we then, and all that kind of thing. It was Miss Maggie who called out to her, 'Children, quieten down, Hannah, what do you mean by that?'

'Better if you take a look, I'm going to move up, but carefully, it's kind of a dead end, I mean it goes on but it doesn't, oh just shuffle up and have a look for yourself.' Hannah shuffled sideways against the wall, 'There's a big chasm, there's nowhere else to go, apart from a ledge here, I'm going to move up slowly so you can take a look'.

'No Hannah, just come back, I will go to the front' Miss Maggie was moving as she spoke, 'No need Miss, look I can just shuffle up,' she disappeared from view. Simon stepped forward, Theo saw him suddenly flail his arms, 'Whoa—!' he yelped, as he teetered dangerously close to the edge, Hannah grabbed his sleeve and yanked him back.

Theo craned his neck to see past the others, but it was hard to see, Miss Maggie, Sarah and then Jack followed Simon and Hannah onto the ledge to the left, there was no more space on that side. Theo and Suhaan both edged out and saw there was another ledge on the right side of the doorway they had come out of, they stepped on to that ledge. 'There's... there's no floor,' Simon said, sounding rather shaky.

They all stood, frozen to the spot looking into nothingness, there was cool air coming up from below them and there was a faint light still coming from the other side across from the chasm, so it meant there was probably something over there. But how on earth where they meant to get there.

'Should we go back to the room we came from?' Jack asked, as no one else was coming up with any ideas. 'Yes, let's do that, we must have missed something, maybe there was a secret exit,' Miss Maggie replied.

Jack was closest from the left side, he started to shuffle back towards the way they had come from, his foot slipped a bit, and he grabbed onto the wall. A strange noise started to come from inside the walls as the stone that Jack's hand had landed on dipped into the wall, and then a stone door came out from nowhere and closed the entrance to the tunnel they had just come through. Suhaan, Theo, Jack and Sarah were all close enough to see what happened.

'Oh boy,' Jack muttered.

Chapter eight

'What's happened, what's happened?' Miss Maggie asked urgently. Sarah was the one to come out of shock and speak up first, 'The path back is blocked Miss Maggie, a door just shut,' she managed to get out before sniffing, like she was about to start crying.

'No way! No, ok fine, ok the way back is closed, ok but now what?' Simon was hyperventilating.

Theo had been studying the chasm for a few minutes, he could feel a breeze, but he still wondered if it was like a 4D effect, 'Do you think it's real, or like an illusion?' Theo finally asked. Suhaan's mouth dropped open on an 'oh' - 'I didn't even think of that, this could totally be like a VR room.

Miss Maggie who had been listening to them tried to be brave and stick a foot out, but quickly changed her mind, safety first she reminded herself, 'Maybe we should drop something and test it,' she suggested. 'Could it be fake, are we being filmed, is this a prank,' Simon, Sarah and Jack were all speaking over each other.

'Shhhh kids, we won't know anything until we test it,' Miss Maggie told them as she clung to the wall with all her strength, too afraid to let go just in case. 'Well, why doesn't just one of us step down and check it?' Jack asked, but everyone gave a loud 'No' to that idea. 'I'll drop my shoe then, shall I?' Jack suggested, to another chorus of 'No' from everyone.

'They have their backpacks with them, why would he suggest his shoe?' whispered Suhaan, who was one of the one's who didn't have his backpack, as he had run off too quickly after Simon and Theo.

'Simon, if you help me stay steady, I can reach and get my bag off, then I can drop something from my bag to test it' Hannah told him. For once, he didn't argue and just did as he was asked, he reached out a hand, and grabbed Hannah's right hand, as she wriggled her bag off from her left side first, brought it down to where they were holding hands and grabbed the strap by letting go of Simon's hand.

She carefully unzipped her bag and felt around until her hand curled around her water bottle, better to use that then risk themselves she thought. Hannah took out her water bottle, then flung it as far away from her as she could. They all watched, they all waited, hoping to hear a loud bang as the bottle landed but sadly it never did, it kept falling, no noise was heard to let them know it had reached the bottom, was there a bottom? It was impossible to guess how far the drop was.

The reality of the danger was sinking in for everyone, 'I think I want to go home now, actually, I know I really want to go home now Miss Maggie, I don't like this' Sarah told Miss Maggie, her voice cracking Miss Maggie looked helplessly around, 'Guys, we can't go back the way we came, we have to try and get across,' she looked over to the other side, it was so far away.

'But there's no more ledge space on my side' Hannah told her, 'How will we go across?'

'Our ledge on this side goes all the way around,

we can make it if we all go this way,' Theo called out excited to have a possible way out of this.

Suhaan checked out the little ledge that worked its way round all the way to the other side of this massive drop, he gulped then gave Theo a nervous grin. 'Kind of living our own adventure now aren't we, not just playing a game, if only we had a few Minecraft weapons eh' Suhaan tried to joke as he slowly started following Theo, not taking his eyes off the ledge to make sure he didn't slip or trip.

The shield on his back was making it a bit hard for Theo to grip the wall behind him, but slowly shuffled across anyway, 'We can do this, just go slow and steady, no rush, keep watching where you put your feet before you step, ok' he told Suhaan, sounding much braver than he felt. He still could not believe or understand how they had ended up here, it really couldn't be part of the museum, so where on earth could they be? Worry about it when I get to the other side, he told himself and just concentrate on shuffling along. He noticed the rest of the group had used the extra space in front of the now closed passage to turn their bodies before stepping onto the ledge they were on, which meant they now faced the wall and could use their hands better to steady themselves, good idea, but not one he was going to risk.

His fingertips were aching from trying to grip the cold and rough wall behind him. His heart thudded in his chest really loudly, he couldn't resist a peek at the drop below him, instantly his stomach lurched, like he was on a roller coaster or something and he felt a bit sick, 'Don't look down kids' Miss Maggie's voice echoed in the big space, he wished he hadn't looked down.

'Bit late for that' Simon muttered loud enough for Theo to hear him; he could empathise with Simon for once.

They had been shuffling at a slow place for a few minutes, with the odd break in silence from a gasp or nervous giggle when Hannah cleared her throat and spoke loudly for everyone to hear her, 'Everyone does realise that we aren't in the museum right,' she didn't sound scared, just matter of fact like she was making a casual observation.

'Not helpful, Hannah,' Miss Maggie told her, wobbling slightly before catching herself. Her feet were longer than the kid's feet, and that meant she had to keep her feet at an angle as they did not fully fit on the ledge otherwise. 'It doesn't make sense to be anywhere but at the museum,' she told

Hannah.

Their voices were carrying over easily to the whole group, echoing in the big space. Theo didn't want to be rude by telling Miss Maggie she was wrong, but it was so obvious to him that she could not be right. 'Miss Maggie, it doesn't make sense that the museum would have a dangerous bottomless pit beneath it, and it doesn't make sense that there was a tornado inside that gallery. If anything, the only thing that might make sense is that we got transported somewhere, you know like wizard of oz, because if this was really a part of the London History Museum then so many people would have sued the Museum by now' he pointed out. If he was right, and he was 98% sure he was right, then they needed to accept the truth and try and find a way out of the real problem, instead of continuing to believe they could still be in the museum.

About halfway to the other side, Theo was shuffling his foot along when his foot caught on a stone and made him falter, sending a few pebbles skittering into the abyss. He froze, arms outstretched for balance.

'What was that?!' Simon yelped.

Heart pounding like someone was going crazy on the drums he was surprised no one else could hear it, Theo tried to keep his voice calm, 'Just a loose rock,' he told them all. He took another careful step, very gently moving up, ok this part was ok again, phew.

'Is the ledge crumbling? Are we all about to die?' Sarah shouted, she stopped moving and everyone behind her had to stop too, 'I can't do this, my hands hurt, my fingers hurt, I'm tired' she complained, saying out loud all the things they were all probably feeling.

'Sarah' Theo said loudly across to her, he and Suhaan had progressed quite a bit from the others now and he was able to see them from where he was, 'I think we're all scared. It's ok to be scared. But you have to carry on, look, if it crumbles, I'm at the front, not you, so you know you can at least get this far safely' at his words Sarah looked over her shoulder, and she realised he was right, they were very close to getting to the end, and Theo was at the front and he was still ok. 'Just take a breather, some deep breaths, wriggle your fingers a bit and then we carry on, ok' Miss Maggie told her gently.

Nodding, Sarah flexed the fingers of one hand, then grabbed the wall again and flexed the other hand, that did feel better. Step by slow step, they continued, their hands had gone cold and numb now, and dirty from clinging onto the rock face. Finally, Theo reached the opening to the other side, he hooked his leg in and twisted his body so he could get off the ledge and be safe. 'Made it!' he called, relief not just in his voice but all through his body, making his knees a bit wobbly as he stood on the firm floor again.

One by one, the others followed, Suhaan practically jumped the last few inches, Jack held out his arm for Theo and Suhaan to help pull him into the opening which looked like a cave mouth. Sarah went limp with relief when she came off, falling to the ground onto her knees, she was closely followed by Miss Maggie and Simon, as Hannah neared the last bit, one foot on the cave opening and the other foot on the ledge, the ledge crumbled with a sharp crack, sending loose stones tumbling into the abyss below.

'Hannah!' Theo shouted.

Her scream pierced the air as she teetered backward, arms flailing. The sudden loss of footing unbalanced her completely, and in an instant, she was falling.

Time seemed to slow. Theo lunged forward, his knees scraping against the jagged ground as he threw himself at the space Hannah had been in. His belly hit the hard earth with a painful thud, but his hand closed around Hannah's wrist just in time.

Her weight yanked at him, her legs kicking wildly over the drop. 'Theo! Don't let me fall, please!' she cried in terror as she hung mid-air.

The pull was stronger than Theo had anticipated. He slid forward, his body dangerously close to the edge. Pebbles skittered under him, dropping into the void.

'Help!' Theo yelled; his voice strained. Miss Maggie was the first to react, grabbing Theo's shoulders with both hands. Suhaan scrambled to his side, gripping Theo's belt and pulling with all his strength.

'Hold on, Theo! We've got you!' Miss Maggie shouted.

With their combined strength, they managed to pull Hannah upwards, 'Just keep a good hold of her,' Miss Maggie gritted through her teeth.

'Hannah, stop moving!' Theo yelled, his grip tightening painfully on her wrist. 'I've got you!'

Hannah froze, her wide eyes locking onto Theo's, she stopped kicking around at nothing and even stopped screaming, just looking straight into Theo's eyes. With a final heave, they managed to drag Hannah back onto solid ground. Hannah immediately scrunched up into a little ball and sat there, rocking backwards and forwards and breathing heavily.

Theo collapsed beside her, his chest heaving. 'You're okay,' he panted, his voice shaky but relieved. 'You're okay.'

'It's over now,' Miss Maggie said gently, crouching beside her. She wrapped an arm around Hannah's shoulders, pulling her close. 'You're safe.' Sarah came over with her water bottle and offered her some water, 'Here, cos you know, you used yours to test the floor for us' she explained. Hannah took a little sip and handed it back, she looked at Miss Maggie, 'It's not over though, is it? We don't know where we are, we don't know how to get home, no one probably knows how to find us. Even if I didn't fall into that pit, are any of us going to be able to go home again?' she asked.

Miss Maggie pulled her phone out of her pocket, 'I'm going to try and call for help, someone will come' she frowned at her phone, Theo could see she had no signal here. She still tried to make a call, but when that failed, she tried to send a message, that didn't deliver. She was gripping her phone so tight, he thought she might crush her phone.

In the heavy silence that hung over the group, the echoes of their frantic rescue seemed to still linger. They felt the reality of Hannah's words and the idea that they may be stuck here was sinking in, no one spoke, and no one moved. It was only when a shadow flitted across the edge of Theo's vision that he realised Jack had been missing, he seemed unbothered by the tension in the air.

'Well,' Jack said, clapping his hands together, 'there are four doorways out there, if we're all still trying to, you know, get out of here.' Everyone turned to look at Jack, Theo's voice was incredulous, 'what you just wandered off for a stroll while we were dealing with a near death? No offense Hannah' he quickly added. Jack looked a bit confused, 'Well what would have been the point of sitting and moping with you lot when I could scout ahead'- Hannah jumped up, her previous sad self long forgotten, 'Scout ahead?!' she shouted, 'Scout ahead? We aren't on a fun camping trip, what if you fell into another chasm, you absolute, argh!' she finished angrily, unable to find the words.

'Like I was saying, I have found four exits, you're welcome' he repeated. His words finally registered for the group, Miss Maggie walked towards Jack, 'Firstly, please don't wander off, secondly good job now show us these exits.' Jack smiled at her and led the way. They all followed Jack who led them to some sort of a central point which just as Jack had told them, had several doors leading off from it.

'Possible unpopular opinion here' Theo spoke, and cleared his throat, 'I think we may have been transported to a tomb in Egypt' he said as he looked at each doorway and the hieroglyph inscription above it.

'Erm hah, that's quite a leap there Theo, I am sure this is a very bad escape room, we just need to follow a path and find our way out' Miss Maggie, was still convinced they were at the museum.

Hannah put a hand on Miss Maggie's arm, 'Miss Maggie, that was not a hologram or a false floor I nearly fell into, I felt the cold coming up from beneath me, and feel the rocks here, look at my scratches, it's not a game Miss, I think Theo is right, that through some impossible way, we are in an actual tomb.'

Miss Maggie's eyes bulged out like an alien for a minute, then she controlled her reaction and patted her hair down, dusted her hands off and smiled a weird smile.

'Why do you think it's a tomb Theo?' Simon asked him. 'Well, I told you about Theodore Hawthorne and that he went missing on a dig in Egypt, he was digging at a place everyone thought was cursed, and the artifacts, this Shield included, the Egyptian museum didn't want to have any of it because they didn't want to be a part of the curse' he told the group. 'I think the curse has somehow brought us into the tomb, I can't explain it but I just kind of have a feeling.'

Miss Maggie stopped doing her freakish smile and shook her head, 'There's no such thing as curses, I think it's all just a terrible escape room under the museum, yes that's what this is. Let's try to pick a doorway, and just work our way out, ok now which door to pick' she was looking at doorways, they all looked the same, dark, cold and very scary.

'They have inscriptions, maybe it says where each path leads' Theo suggested helpfully.

'Yes, good idea, ok, so we've just come through that way, so it doesn't matter what it says, we can ignore it, that one in the middle says nothing. This one has a coiled snake, and that one has a vulture, who remembers any of the symbols we looked at before lunch?' She asked the group.

'Those two mean danger, the vulture we saw and the coiled snake my grandpa told me about it' Theo spoke up, Hannah took out her sheet from her bag, 'I think he is right about danger for the vulture, I don't have anything for snake thing, oh oh I do have that Dog and a shield, it means protector of a tomb maybe', 'No' Theo cut her off, 'That's not a dog, that's a Jackal linked to Anubis, the underworld and mummification' he told the group, remembering what his grandpa had taught him.

'Right, let's go through the one with nothing and go from there' Miss Maggie exclaimed and started walking towards it. She paused when she noticed Theo was not moving, 'Come on Theo' she urged. But Theo shook his head no, 'I want to go and put this shield back and I think it should go into the room with the Jackal, it does have a Jackal on it, look' he told them, turning around so they could all take a look at the shield that was strapped to his back. 'You guys go through the blank door, but I need to go and do this. If this is an escape room and you get out first, then just let someone know to come and find me' he told her and headed for the jackal with the shield path. Suhaan followed behind, and Hannah looked at Miss Maggie, 'Sorry, I'm going with them, he saved my life, he knows the hieroglyphs and I don't think this is an escape room,' she told the teacher before running behind the boys.

Sarah looked unsure as to what to do, 'I'm going with Miss Maggie, probably better to not go into a room that has horrible meanings, better to pick the one with nothing right?' she hurried off, Simon looked at Jack, they looked at the passage that Theo had taken 'He does seem to know what the pictures mean, but then we should probably stay with an adult, what do you think?' Simon asked Jack, Jack was about to follow Theo but then he saw Miss Maggie pull out her phone to use as a torch while Theo, Suhaan and Hannah seemed to walk into the pitch-black nothingness. 'Ah I'm going where it's not scary and dark' he told Simon and ran off behind the girls, Simon following behind him…

Chapter nine

Theo, Suhaan and Hannah carefully made their way through the very dark passage; they didn't have Miss Maggie's phone light this time. They had their hands out, touching the sides of the passage, and shuffled slowly, trying to be very careful about taking small steps.

'Thanks for believing in me guys, and Hannah, I um, I'm sorry for chewing your donuts' he told her quietly.

She paused for a second feeling the sting from her scraped knees and elbows, remembering how he had thrown himself to the floor to catch her, 'I'm sorry for being mean to you too Theo, I just hope we get out of here and maybe we can try to not be mean to each other' she suggested. 'Not that anyone asked me, but it sounds like a good plan,' Suhaan butted in, making them laugh.

The three of them shuffled along in the dark a few more steps when Hannah asked; 'So do you really think we've landed up in a cursed tomb somehow?'

Theo slowed down, almost stopping, he knew it must sound like a crazy idea, but he had to be honest with them, 'It's the only thing that makes sense you know, like we haven't even talked about the tornado in the room that happened, when is that ever normal? And if there was an escape room under the museum, don't you think someone would have spilled their guts about it and it would be an open secret, and' he continued, now on a roll, 'And, don't you think the museum would have been sued if someone got hurt in an escape room, and look at you, you're hurt, that abyss or chasm whatever you want to call it, it was real.'

'You know that all makes sense when you think about it like this, but if we are in a tomb, how on earth do we get back home?' Suhaan asked.

'Well let's be logical' Hannah told them. 'So, we agree we think we are in a tomb, a cursed tomb maybe if Theo is right, we have something from the tomb that was in the museum, what if it's like a key, what if by putting it back, it sends us back home?' she suggested.

Theo and Suhaan turned to look at where Hannah's voice had come from, as they couldn't really see her in the dark, 'That tracks you know, and it's the only theory we have, we give back what does not belong to us, what started this mess for us and maybe the tomb will spit us back out to where we belong. Yeh, good thinking Hannah' he told her. 'Stay close. And don't push any stones in with your hands. You remember what happened last time with Jack, we don't need another door slamming shut behind us,' Theo warned them.

In the quiet they could hear their feet scraping on the floor, and even every breath they were taking, 'It's so quiet... too quiet. I feel like something's watching us,' Hannah spoke nervously.

'Maybe it's just the Jackal from the door. You know, waiting to pounce on us and drink our blooooood' Suhaan told them, trying to make jokes, but Hannah did not find it funny. 'Not funny, and not accurate and not appropriate' she told him.

As they approached the end of the passage,

their footsteps got slower, they were afraid of what they might find, thankfully this chamber had some glowing hieroglyphs on the wall so they could at least look around. It looked like an empty room, across the room was another archway leading off from the room, it looked like they simply had to walk across to the other side. Theo poked a foot out and tested the floor, it was solid, ok that's good.

'Guys, focus. It looks like a connecting room. There's another passage across from here, but I have a horrible feeling it's not as easy as it looks, so go slow and steady.' Theo continued to look around the small room, suspiciously.

Suhaan copied Theo and tested the ground in front of him before stepping out of the passage and into the room, he came up next to Theo putting a hand on his shoulder, 'Relax Theo, what's the worst that could—'A faint click echoed beneath Suhaan's foot.

They all froze, and the smile vanished from Suhaan's face. The sound of grinding stone filled the room, they looked at the doorway across the room expecting it to shut, but no, the grinding noise continued and then suddenly a spear shot out from one of the walls. It flew across the room from left to right, there was more grinding of stone as another spear shot out, this time from the right side of the room going to hit the wall on the left, it was just in front of them like a warning shot. Hannah had stopped moving, only her eyes moved, 'Are you guys ok' she asked slowly.

'Ah yeh, but let's all just be still for a minute. No moving, no stepping,' he told the other two as he tried to think what to do. Bending down on the spot, Theo tried to take a close look at the slab he was standing on, the floor was made up of square slabs, he took a long look at the one he was standing on then turned to look at the one Hannah was standing on and lastly compared it to the one Suhaan had stepped on. He didn't know what he was looking for, just something, anything to give a clue.

'I think I know what you're looking for,' Hannah spoke up. 'What is he looking for?' Suhaan asked urgently, he had been holding his breath until now, trying not to move at all.

'The slabs that Theo and I are standing on match the colour of the stone on the wall, but the slab that you are standing on, is slightly off colour.

I think if we step on just the wall-coloured slabs, we might be ok' she told them.

'It's the best idea, it's kind of the only option we have, let's do it' Suhaan told them.

Theo was at the front of their little trio, Hannah was right about the difference in colour of the slabs, and Suhaan was right, they didn't have another option but to go with the best option they had. He tried to make his step as big as possible so they would step on less slabs. Nothing happened on his first step, or his second, he was just one step away from the other end, but he paused. 'What's the matter', Hannah asked from behind him.

Theo looked at the slabs really closely, 'I can't tell which one is safe, they all look a bit off colour to me' he told them.

Hannah bent low to the ground, looking intently, 'I can't tell either. Should we just take a risk and run for it?' she suggested.

'Too risky, I think if we try a jump from here, we should be able to reach the end.' Theo looked to Hannah and Suhaan to see if they were on board with his plan, Hannah looked at Suhaan, who shrugged his shoulders at her, they waited and watched as Theo stood on the edge of his safe slab, then took a step and a leap, launching himself onto the other side. He made it!

Suhaan jumped onto the slab that Theo had just left empty, he copied Theo and made it across, and last Hannah jumped from her slab, to Suhaan's old one, then to Theo's old one and took a huge jump to the other side.

They all laughed nervously from the thrill of having managed to do that in one piece with nothing else going wrong. 'Ok, this bit all seems to be the same colour through out so should be safe.' Theo looked at the floor where they had all landed, it was hard to see as it was another passage with no lights, squinting he spoke 'We should be ok.' This bit was wide enough for them all to stand side by side, they all stepped forward confidently but before they knew what was happening, the floor beneath their feet gave way and all three children fell with a whoosh, landing on something hard. And small. And round.

Chapter ten

Miss Maggie led Simon, Sarah, and Jack through the dark and damp smelling passage. The air was heavy, carrying a stale, earthy scent that clung to their nostrils. 'This passage smells like when I found an old packet of bread and took it out, it was all green on the bottom and smelt really earthy, like this' Jack told the group.

'Tell the truth Jack, you only realised it was green when you took a bite, after toasting and buttering it!' Simon added, remembering the story as he had been at Jack's house. The laughter from the boys helped squash some of the tension and created an almost normal feeling for a minute, but that feeling soon left as the narrow corridor felt like it was closing in on them, getting narrower.

'Remind me never to sign up for a trip again' murmured Sarah.

'How about next time we don't go into rooms that say keep out,' Miss Maggie told them all 'anyway we'll be out of this passage soon,' she hoped they would be out soon, her palm was sweating from holding the phone up to see where they were going, and she felt this strange shiver through her body, like the adrenalin had worn off and she was fighting to stay upright.

The tunnel path was coming to an end and up ahead they could see a room coming into view. There were no hieroglyphs on the wall of this room unlike the first chamber they woke up in, this room looked like it was deliberately being kept dark.

The air grew colder with each step, like there was a chill that was coming off from the stones themselves. Long scary shadows were being cast from the light of the little phone torch, making everything look jagged, sharp and spooky. At the centre of the room, was a large and elaborate stone sarcophagus. It was massive, much bigger than it needed to be surely? It sat on a sunken level, but still it commanded all the attention of the room. Wide stone steps led down to it, their edges were rough like they had not been used. The sound of their breathing seemed muffled, as if the room itself was swallowing the noise, refusing to let anything escape.

A strange energy hummed around it, a low and almost imperceptible sound, but it was making the hairs on their arms and the backs of their necks rise. Everything here felt wrong, it made Miss Maggie's stomach twist with dread just being in this room.

'Is that... a coffin?' Jack asked, his voice trembling.' Will a vampire come out of it?'

'It's a sarcophagus,' Miss Maggie corrected, her voice quivered. They all stood rooted to the spot at the entrance, 'It's ancient, and why would a vampire suddenly come out of an ancient Egyptian sarcophagus?' Simon questioned Jack as he edged forward, peering in, 'I think we should just go back, pick another door, we don't want to wake up whatever is inside that' he whispered and pointed to the sarcophagus.

Miss Maggie didn't answer, her entire focus was drawn to the sarcophagus looming before. Its surface gleamed faintly under her light, the carved images and symbols on the sides seeming to almost ripple and shift. No that had to be a trick of the light. She crouched and squinted trying to get a good look at hieroglyph near the base.

'Guardian something something bound danger? That symbol is danger and that one I think is consequences...'

A chill snaked down her spine, so cold and sudden it felt like someone, or something had run its cold fingers down her spine. She backed away quickly, her face pale.

'No,' she said sharply, her voice louder than she intended, 'this isn't the right way,' she said firmly, her voice a little too loud. 'We shouldn't be here. Let's go back.' Something about this room felt horribly alive and she didn't think they should spend any unnecessary time in here, she started backing out.

Sarah and Jack looked at each other, they had questions, but seeing the look on Miss Maggie's scared face, they decided it was not a good time to hang about here asking questions. Jack reached out and held Sarah's hand, trying to help her back out quickly.

Miss Maggie whirled around, her expression

stern. 'Maybe I read that wrong' she said with a nervous laugh, 'It probably doesn't say danger at all, but I was thinking, seeing as it's a very dark room, why don't we head back eh, try another route, that might be a good idea' she tried to reassure the kids.

Miss Maggie held her phone up to light the path and ushered them all out of the room as quickly as she could, she turned back to take a look at the sarcophagus again and felt those cold fingers down her spine again. Shaking the weird feeling off, she hurried behind the kids to get out of there as fast as possible. The group retraced their steps, Simon kept looking behind him, to make sure some mummy didn't suddenly come out and start following them. No one spoke until they reached the passage's entrance, where they paused to catch their breath.

'Where do you think we are, Miss Maggie, do you think this is a tomb now like Theo said?' Sarah asked.

Miss Maggie sighed and leaned against the wall, taking off her glasses to rub her temples. 'I don't know, Sarah. All I can be sure of is that we are definitely not in the museum.'

Simon frowned. 'So... hang on' he began, his voice unsteady as he looked at the others. 'We're in some kind of underground cave or tomb and are you saying we aren't even in London anymore?' His voice rising at the end.

Sarah wrapped her arms around herself, 'This can't be real' she whispered, 'Maybe we all hit our heads in the museum and are in some shared weird dream' she tried to explain. Miss Maggie looked at the children with some pity and sadness, 'Unfortunately it seems that we are in tomb or cave,' Miss Maggie admitted reluctantly. 'But we'll find our way out. We just need to stay calm and stick together.'

Jack looked around at the doors, 'Should we flip a coin or something to see which way to take?' he asked, each path looking equally scary.

Simon hesitated, 'Whatever way we choose, could be as bad or worse than that pit we came across.'

The children all looked to Miss Maggie, who pasted on a fake smile, 'Let's just go through here, if we don't like it, we can come back and try another path, the main thing to keep in mind is to be careful, ok. Now let's see what do we have here, a vulture or just a bird flying, right, can't be too bad, and I don't think they are revealing the correct information as it is. I say we just go this way, follow me' she told the kids as she led them through the next passage.

The new passage was wider but that didn't make it less scary. It wasn't as dark somehow; they realised why when they got to the end. The room it led to was nothing like the one they had just come out of. Hieroglyphs covered every inch of the walls, glowing faintly with an otherworldly light that pulsated, as if the room was breathing. The room was also not empty.

The walls were lined with rows of life-sized stone soldiers, each one standing rigidly at attention. Each soldier held a weapon – spear, sword, shield – all carved with so much detail that it made them look almost real and sharp enough to use. Their stone faces were also hauntingly real, they had wrinkles and scars as though someone had poured cement over real men to trap them for eternity.

'What is this place?' Jack whispered, in the heavy silence, his voice bounced off the walls startling them all.

Miss Maggie put her phone away and looked around, 'It's... a guard room,' she said slowly. 'Or at least, that's what it looks like.'

Her mind raced, trying to piece together what it all could mean, a forbidden tomb warning people away with a guard room to perhaps to scare looters or something more sinister, like keeping people in? This was not the tomb of a revered or loved pharaoh, more like, as Theo had tried to tell her, a cursed tomb. She felt her throat go dry.

'Ok, hurry now, look there's another door on the other side, just carefully get past these statues and maybe we can find a way out' she told the children.

They all stopped looking at the soldiers along the walls and stepped into the centre of the room when a grinding noise filled the room, low and relentless, like the groaning of a giant. The sound reverberated through the entire room, making the glowing hieroglyphs shimmer and pulse. All four of them huddled together in the centre looking around, trying to see where the noise was coming from. 'I watched a film once; it had stone soldiers who came to life' Jack told them. 'Don't jinx us by telling us that now Jack' Simon warned him. But the soldiers did not move, they remained frozen, their eyes still blank. The grinding noise grew louder, almost deafening now.

Miss Maggie grabbed Sarah's arm and told them all to hold hands, 'Let's quickly try to get to the other side and get out.' She barely finished speaking when the grinding noise changed, becoming a deep guttural rumble. Around them the walls began to shift, slowly at first, so subtly, but then faster pressing forward. The motion made it look like the soldiers were coming at them to attack.

'The soldiers! They're alive!' shrieked Sarah, 'No, it's the walls, they're moving in on us' Simon shouted. The doorways had already been closed off to them from the walls moving in, even the ceiling was coming down on them now.

'There's no space! Theres no space!' Jack cried, as they were all being squished from all sides. Their arms were now pinned by their sides, Miss Maggie was tilting her head at an odd angle due to the ceiling having come down on them.

'I can't breath, I can't get enough air into me' Simon was saying, it was clear he was on the cusp of a panic attack and there wasn't anything any of them could do.

Jack was facing Miss Maggie, he looked at her with so much sadness, 'I don't want this to be the end, Miss, not like this' he managed as a single tear rolled down his cheek, Maggie started to cry now too, this wasn't fair, this couldn't be their fate.

The grinding stopped, for a terrifying heartbeat there was only silence, then with an awful lurch and groan the floor gave way. The ground crumbled beneath their feet, and they all plummeted into darkness.

Chapter eleven

Looking around Hannah's breath caught in her throat as she scrambled to her knees, her hands sinking into a pile of cold hard coins, she gasped then, the sound echoing faintly in the massive room. They had landed on what looked like an enormous pile of gold coins, glittering and cold and just so many of them. And all around them lay treasures like Alladin's cave, goblets with jewels, emeralds and rubies, gold and pearl necklaces, just so many things.

'Wow... it's like something out of a dream.' Hannah said as she picked up some coins in her hands and let them fall out like a waterfall of gold coins.

'Or a movie. Look at all this stuff! We're rich!' Suhaan told her.

'Don't touch anything. It's probably all cursed!' Theo hissed, holding his hands up like he was trying to ward off some invisible evil. 'Let's just try and return-'

'Who dares to enter here?' A voice boomed through the room, it was deep and terrifying. Hannah and Suhaan huddled closer to Theo as they looked around, looking for who the voice belonged to.

Hannah pointed a shaky finger to one of the many pillars in the room, 'M-might be hiding behind a pillar' she whispered. The trio looked around them looking for something, anything, to use as a weapon. Theo took the shield off his back and held it up in front of him protectively, he felt terrified, but he would not give up easily. Hannah spotted a sceptre which she grabbed and held defensively in front of her, and then there was Suhaan. He crouched down, scooping up a handful of gold coins. Theo gave him an incredulous look, 'What on earth are you doing?' Suhaan held up a coin, 'Throwing stars, duh!' Theo shook his head, 'Seriously dude?' he asked, he was going to say more but he felt a shift around him then, like the room suddenly felt colder.

Out of the corner of his eye, Theo saw it – a faint shimmer, like heat rising off a hot road, he turned his head sharply toward it, his hands gripping the shield.

'Uh, guys…' he began, not taking his eyes off the shimmery thing he was looking at. Hannah and Suhaan followed his gaze, their eyes widening as the shimmer began to grow. It flickered and wavered, like a TV screen glitching, the static morphing slowly into a humanoid shape.

Without hesitation, Suhaan threw a coin at the shimmery shape—It passed right through and hit the wall.

'Guys, I think we should-' Theo started but Hannah beat him to it, 'Run! We should Run!' she shouted as she headed away from the ghostly shape that was forming.

The boys turned and followed her, they ran darting this way and that way as they searched for an escape. The trap door they had fallen through loomed high above their heads, no chance of climbing up to there to escape. They continued running aimlessly, weaving between scattered piles of gold coins. Out of breath, Suhaan doubled over and gasped, 'We can't play 'you're it' with a ghost, guys – we need a plan!' As if in response, the ghost blurred with unnatural speed, appearing directly in their path. They all skidded to a stop and shrieked 'AAAGGGH' at the same time.

'Stop that noise, it hurts my ears' The ghost complained. The ghost's voice, sharp but eerily human, Theo and Suhaan stopped shrieking, but Hannah let out a few shrieks that just didn't want to end yet, 'Ah..Ah..ah..huh?' she ended in confusion, wondering why the boys were not screaming anymore.

Theo stared at the ghost, frozen in disbelief, his lips moved silently for a second, like he had forgotten how to say words. 'You're, you're Theodore Hawthorne' he finally managed to speak as he recognised the man from the pictures Harold had shown him. The name hung in the air, heavy and full of more questions than answers.

The ghost stood there in faded khaki trousers and a once white shirt, now yellowed and ghostly see through. He also had on a wide brimmed hat which looked ridiculous in this room. Everything about him said 'I'm from the olden days' – but here he was, a ghost.

Hearing his name he snapped his head at Theo

in shock, 'You know my name' his eyes narrowed at the kids in suspicion, 'How?'

Theo tried not to let on how scared he was, he stood his ground and answered as clearly as he could, even though all he could manage now was a whisper. 'I've seen your photos…on your dig and with my grandpa.'

The ghost's expression flickered and he glitched in and out, he looked surprised, confused and something else. He took a small step closer to Theo, 'Your grandpa?' he asked, clearly trying to figure out how this child's grandpa would know him.

Thoedore Hawthorne's ghost stared at the three children; his sadness seemed to affect the atmosphere of the room making it feel heavier. He took in their bright clothes and backpack, he swallowed, his throat felt dry, funny he had never wanted for food or drink since he ended up here and today, he felt different.

'What year is it?' he asked at last, his voice trembling with dread and hesitation, as he both wanted to know but didn't want his worst fears confirmed either.

Suhaan, ever ready to provide an answer, piped up, '2024. It's been ages since you went missing,' He paused for dramatic effect before adding brightly, 'Oh and Theo here, well he's your great-grandson by the way.'

The words hit him like actual blows, Theodore's ghostly knees buckled, and he dropped onto a pile of coins. He leaned forward, his elbows resting on his knees as he covered his face with both his hands, as if he was trying to block out the information and the truth.

'Great-grandson' he whispered hoarsely, 'My goodness…it's been so long' His hands fell away, Theo could see some glistening near his eyes, like ghostly tears. He felt quite bad for the Theodore ghost then, 'So my little Harold grew up. He had a family of his own, it's all rather quite overwhelming, do forgive me, I need a moment' he told the kids as he sat there in deep thought.

Theo cautiously stepped closer to Theodore, nothing in his life had prepared him to come face to face with the ghost of his ancestor. 'My grandpa told me a bit about you, about your expedition, and that you vanished in Egypt without a trace, what happened to you?' he asked, trying to make sense of this mystery.

Theo, Suhaan and Hannah all seemed to be no longer scared of being faced with a ghost and all gathered closer to hear what Theodore had to say. Theodore looked up but his mind seemed to be far away, as if he was drawing on the events from a far away place, finally he spoke.

'It was 1923,' he began slowly, 'My father, that would be your great-great-grandfather, Reginald, we were in Egypt. I had uncovered the location of this tomb, people said to stay away, but you see I had found it by accident as a child and ever since then it had driven me crazy to try and find it again, find out all about it.'

'I read your notebook, it said you almost gave up looking just before you found this place' Theo interrupted, Theodore nodded. He gave a small humourless laugh, 'yes, we almost gave up until I fell into the burial room and then found this room. No one else would enter, took me ages to take out pieces one by one, but when I said I wanted to open the sarcophagus, that's what did it. They called it cursed, they insisted we leave it undisturbed; I was convinced it was all just superstition; I dismissed their warnings.'

Theodore fell silent, remembering the events, 'I had sent some items back with my father, I could see being here was not good for his health, but he wouldn't complain, so I convinced him the artifacts needed to be escorted by him back to the UK. I was meant to oversee the dismantling of the site, but I couldn't. It was like the sarcophagus was calling to me, I swear to this day I could hear a whisper, like my name on the wind, it was driving me crazy, so I headed back down, one last time I told myself.' Theodore paused again, shaking his head at the memory.

'What happened when you returned?' asked Theo, fully absorbed in the story. 'I returned with a crowbar, chisels, a mallet – everything I needed to pry that lid open. It wasn't easy…the lid was massive, heavier than I had anticipated, but like I said, I was driven by this crazy need.'

He glanced at Theo, his eyes shadowed, 'It wasn't just a normal curiosity, I was consumed by need. I battled with that lid, pushing and pulling and hammering away at it, I thought I felt a slip, like it gave a little, but that's when my lantern started flickering, there was no draft in that room, but my lantern wouldn't stop flickering. Then I heard it,' he was breathing heavily, like talking about it was taking a toll on him, like he was back there that day re-living it.

Suhaan moved a step closer, 'Heard what?' he asked.

'The whispers. Soft, hissing voices, like a hundred voices chanting at the same time, murmuring, but no one else was there, just me. My lantern was giving next to no light by then, I felt a presence, like I was being watched.' Theodore's voice dropped; he was now trembling as he recounted that moment. 'The chanting whispers grew louder, I couldn't understand them, they were in a different language I knew that much, the more the chants grew, the more I felt like I was suffocating in that room. But I was so foolish, none of it was enough to make me stop, I felt like was desperate to see what was inside that stone coffin. I gripped the crowbar tighter, and I pushed my full weight against the lid.' He flexed his ghostly fingers around an unseen crowbar, his muscle memory tightening his grip, 'When I thought I might make the lid shift I felt a powerful force, unseen, slam into me. It hurled me across the chamber, my back hit the stone wall. I managed to get up, but I was lifted off my feet like a ragdoll and thrown again, but this time not against the wall, it felt like I was thrown into nothing' he stopped his breathing heavy.

'What do you mean?' Theo asked, not understanding how you can be thrown into nothing.

`I mean' Theodore continued, 'I felt as if the ground beneath me vanished. There was no up or down as everything had gone dark, I felt weightless like I was floating, suspended in darkness. I don't know how long I was there in that nothingness, all I had was a sense of falling. When I woke up, I was here' he gestured all around him.

Suhaan's brow furrowed, 'So why didn't you just leave?'

Theodore's laugh was hollow, 'Leave? Chance would be a fine thing boy, don't you think I tried? Believe me, I tried. The moment I woke up here I headed for the exit, but the room fought back. The room doesn't let me leave. No matter what I have tried, I am always just, here' he finished sadly.

The room fell into an uneasy silence, the weight of his words pressing heavily on them all. 'And now you've come here, consumed by the same greed for treasure like me'- 'No! not at all!' Hannah told him indignantly.

'We didn't come searching for anything, we got transported here' Theo added, as Hannah furiously nodded.

'Transported? But how?' he demanded.

Theo, Suhaan and Hannah exchanged uneasy glances. Theo sighed and rubbed his head, 'Well, we have a theory' he began. 'We were in the London History Museum – that's were your artifacts are kept by the way. Anyway, I picked up this shield, something…happened. It started vibrating and a tornado appeared inside a room, and we ended up here. I know it sounds a bit fantastical,' Theodore raised an eyebrow at this, 'fantastical, really, you say this as you speak to a ghost.'

Hannah chimed in, 'We think that if Theo returns the shield to wherever you took it from, maybe we can be transported back to where we came from. And well…stealing from the dead is wrong, you know' She gave Theodore a pointed look, one which had Theodore look down in embarrassment.

Theodore jumped up and clapped his hands, 'But this is fantastic, putting that shield back might not just return you, it might break the curse on me and finally release me from here too. I had been thinking about the very same thing not long ago, maybe a few days, or was it a few years ago? Who knows, time is difficult to grasp here.' He gestured toward Theo, his voice softening, 'Let me see the shield boy.' Reluctantly, Theo held it out. Theodore approached, his movement careful, as though he was a bit afraid of the shield. 'Ah yes, I remember it well.'

'This shield is believed to have belonged to Pharaoh Amunotep's special guard. He was the one who organised the movement with the priests to punish the traitor, Nakht-Ankh.'

This made no sense to Theo, 'Erm, if the shield belonged a special guard, why was it buried with a traitor?' he asked, 'And how did you find all this out?'

Theodore's ghostly form flickered in and out for a minute, before he stabilised again and explained 'This shield, it was gifted by Amunotep to his special guard, a symbol of the Pharaohs trust, but, the unfortunate guard failed at his task. Unable to protect Amunotep from the conspiracy which led to the cursed one over throwing Amunotep. The guard, overcome with guilt and shame, in an act of penance asked for this shield to be buried here with the guardian of the afterlife, who was supposed to keep watch and keep the cursed one bound to this tomb.'

Suhaan looked confused, 'Wait, how do you even know all this though? Did someone drop their history book in here to keep you entertained?' he asked.

Theodore chuckled, it seemed to shake around the whole chamber, 'Not quite a history book, young man. When I realised, I couldn't leave the treasure chambers, I explored them thoroughly and found several scrolls, tucked away, hidden in secret compartments. So many of the artifacts were documented. The story of the treachery, the purpose of each artifact – all written down. I have no idea how long it took me to decipher the language and understand it, like I said, no concept of time down here. All I know is, I found everything I had set out to find, but at what cost? Too high a cost,' he shook his head.

Chapter twelve

Theodore seemed to shake himself out of the sad feelings that had surrounded him, 'Come on then' he told the kids. He beckoned them forward, 'I can show you where it goes, the guards shield, we can test your theory, see if it does the trick. Who knows it might be a case of you put it back and bob's your uncle' he told them. Suhaan turned to Theo, 'you never said anything about having an uncle called Bob'.

'That's because I don't,' Theo replied.

'Stop wasting time guys, right Mr. ghost please lead the way, show us where to put this shield back and hopefully put an end to this totally horrible day' Hannah instructed Theodore.

Theodore glided effortlessly ahead, the three

children followed behind, their footsteps making noise as they stepped on and over various bits of gold. He led them past several pillars, all had hieroglyphs showing stories of greed and consequences which the children did not understand or pay much attention to. At last, they approached a low archway, it was hidden in shadow, its edges smoothed by time.

This new chamber was very different to the treasure room they had just been in. there was light, an otherworldly light and they couldn't find the source for it. 'Don't touch the walls, just to be safe, all those hieroglyphs in this room, well they are curses. Learnt the hard way to respect them' Theodore told them. The room suddenly felt dangerous, as if there was a weight pressing down on everything from centuries of secrets and magic.

At the centre of the room looked the jackal statue, its sheer size was dominating the space. The gold statue gleamed, its surface polished to a mirror-like sheen that caught the weird light of the room and reflected it in fractured rays across the rest of the room. The Jackal's eyes seemed to follow them, that couldn't be right, Theo moved further to the left, then to the right to test this, they definitely seemed to follow him.

The Jackal looked like it had the body of a bodybuilder, with bulging muscles, he had a sword in one hand and looked like the other hand was supposed to be holding a shield, the shield that Theo was holding, which suddenly felt uncomfortable in his hands. It stood atop a raised platform, 'Those symbols on the platform' Theodore pointed out like some tour guide, 'Well they are protective symbols, and symbols of power, which are supposed to allow him to keep the cursed one bound for eternity' he explained.

Now that they were closer, Theo could see it wasn't a normal sword, it was a colossal sword is the only way Theo could describe it. Suhaan was pulling on his arm, 'Look at this, just look, we need a sword like this for Minecraft.' It was long, it curved near the end and became wider there too then tapered to a sharp point, when they got closer to it, Theo could have sworn that there was a magical hum coming from the sword. The room had lots of other ceremonial weapons, spears, other smaller shields with cobras on them, there were some jars and smaller statues at the base of the dais that the Jackal was standing on.

'This' Theodore said softly, 'is the Guardian. This statue, it's not just a monument, think of him like the prison warden. Forever awake, forever alert so that the cursed one may never leave.' Theo shivered, 'It's huge' he murmured, he felt tiny next to it.

'That is where the shield belongs' Theodore added, pointing to the Jackal's extended arm. Theo turned to Theodore, 'Here, you took it, so you get to return it' he tried to shove the shield into Theodore's hands, but it just passed right through.

'I can't' he told Theo, his ghostly form flickering again, 'It's part of the curse I think, I haven't been able to hold any of this in my hands. Can plant my bottom on it to have a seat, but when I try to touch anything of value, nothing.'

Theo sighed, staring up at the golden guardian. 'It's massive, I won't be able to get up there without a boost' he told Suhaan. 'If we both actually climb up to that ledge there' he said pointing to the platform the Jackal was standing on, 'then you can give me a leg up.'

Suhaan was rolling up his sleeves and trying to map out his route to the platform. It was Hannah that helped, she saw him eyeing it up hesitantly. 'Look, there's grooves and patterns everywhere that you can use as grips and points to place your feet' she told them helpfully.

Theo and Suhaan wiped their palms on their trousers to get ready, then both approached the statue. The climb was slow and difficult, while the carvings provided some grip, the gold was so smooth, it was very slippery. Theo felt his muscles strain, the climbing wall felt easy compared to this, note to self never complain about the climbing wall again he thought.

By the time both boys reached the ledge, they were red faced and sweating. Theo turned to Suhaan, bracing himself on the statue, 'Okay, I'll need that boost now please, just keep steady while you do it' he told Suhaan.

Suhaan crouched, interlocking his hands to form a foothold, Theo waited for Suhaan to be ready, then placed a foot in Suhaan's hands and gripped the statue for balance. With a heave, Suhaan hoisted him upward.

The Jackal's golden arm loomed just above his head, he tried to avoid its eyes, he knew it wasn't alive, but it was still very scary. 'I'm going to take the shield off now, are you ok down there?' he asked Suhaan, letting him know to expect some movement.

'I'm good, you just get on with it' grunted Suhaan, straining under the weight of holding up Theo. Carefully Theo jiggled the shield off his shoulders, holding the Jackal's arm with one hand for balance, he looped the strap of the shield onto the Jackal's arm. The moment the shield settled into position; the chamber seemed to take a breath. A low hum resonated through the air. They waited, but nothing else was happening, 'ok, you better come down, can't keep you up for much longer' Suhaan groaned. Theo quickly slid down to stand next to Suhaan on the platform, they watched the Jackal, but other than the hum, there was absolutely nothing else happening. The boys jumped down from the platform, feeling dejected, 'Well that was a big old pile of nothing' commented Theodore, looking as sad as the trio felt.

'No point hanging around here, might as well go and sit on piles of gold coins to at least feel better about this' Suhaan suggested. Nodding, they all headed back through the archway and into the treasure room. Hannah rubbed her scraped arms thoughtfully, 'Maybe we're missing something, or maybe we just had it wrong and will be stuck here now, like him' she said pointing to Theodore.

Suhaan plonked down on his pile of gold and picked up a goblet that was near him, he pretended to say cheers to Hannah and then pretended to drink from it. Hannah looked over at Theo who shook his head, clearly Suhaan was slowly losing the plot he thought. He could understand it, there didn't seem to be a way out, he suddenly remembered the others. 'Guys we need to go and find the others, we should regroup.'

Theodore blinked in surprise, 'Others? There are more of you?' he asked.

'Yeh' Theo replied absently, looking up at the gaping hole through which they had landed into this room, 'There's Miss Maggie, Simon, Sarah and Jack. We split up when the floor'-

Suhaan waved a hand at hole 'When we came crashing down into this useless treasure room. No offence Theodore' he told the ghost.

All three of the children stared up at the jagged opening in the ceiling through which they had fallen.

'Why may I ask, are we all looking up there?' Theodore asked them as he too peered into the dark opening.

'Because we're trying to figure out a way of how to climb back up' Hannah told him in a matter-of-fact way.

Theodore casually looked down at his ghostly nails pretending to blow on them 'Well if it was up to me, I would prefer to take the stairs over climbing into a dark hole with no rope or ladder' he told them. Three heads turned to look at him and three pairs of eyes bored into him, 'What stairs would you take Theodore?' asked Theo.

The ghost floated over to one of the many pillars in the room, reached around and tapped a hidden panel, 'I did tell you I can't touch the gold, but it seems I can touch anything that isn't gold, including the secret trap door in this pillar' he told them, feeling rather pleased with himself.

'Theodore, you the man!' Suhaan told him as he excitedly got to his feet and ran over to the pillar, 'This is great, thank you,' Suhaan told him, Hannah and Theo thanked him too as they wasted no time in starting to climb up the narrow staircase. It was a spiral staircase, and as with all the tunnels and passageways here, it was dark. Theo paused mid step, cautiously bringing his foot down 'Hey did you guys hear that?' he asked. They all listened, there it was again, 'That's voices' Hannah told them, 'And it sounds like our lot', they started to climb faster.

Chapter thirteen

'Help!' The faint cry echoed down to them, followed by a muffled 'we're stuck!'

Theo's heart raced, 'It's them'. As they reached the top of the staircase, they could see a dim light swinging around, it was the light from Miss Maggie's phone. As their eyes adjusted to the dim light, Hannah gasped and froze. Suspended above a bed of spikes, trapped in a net, were Miss Maggie, Simon, Jack and Sarah, all a tangle of arms and legs. 'What happened to you lot?' Suhaan asked, they all tried to look at the direction of Suhaan's voice and the net started swaying like crazy.

'Am I glad to see you guys for once in my life' Simon told them happily.

'Oh Theo, Hannah, Suhaan, you're all ok, that's brilliant' Miss Maggie spoke through a mouthful of rope, her face was squished into the net.

'We have been nearly killed, again, and again and again, we were squeezed in a room where the walls came in on us and then whoosh, we fell through, only to be trapped into this net' Jack complained.

'Oh we fell through a floor too, but we fell onto a pile of gold coins and found the ghost of Theodore Hawthorne' Suhaan told them conversationally. 'You found treasure' 'whaat, there's a ghost' 'awesome' they all seemed to speak at once, over one another.

'Can you help get us down somehow?' Miss Maggie asked. Theo looked at Suhaan, 'I'm going to run down to get a spear from the treasure room, keep an eye on them' he told Suhaan and ran down the stairs back down to the treasure room.

Ghostly Theodore was standing at the foot of the stairs, 'What's happening, I heard lots of noise but couldn't make anything out.' 'We found the others, they're stuck in a net, I need – ah that' he said as he grabbed a spear and a small gold dagger. 'Brb' he told Theodore and rushed off.

'Brb, what is brb?' he heard the ghostly voice of Theodore call up to him. He didn't have time to stop and explain, rushing back up the stairs he was a bit out of breath when he reached the rest of the group.

'Right' he said, 'I'm going to hold this spear out, and Jack, you're the closest, try to extend your arm and grab it, we can then pull you all closer. And then I got this dagger to cut you out' he told them.

Theo held the spear out, Jack reached out, he stretched, his fingers, they just about bushed the tip of the spear, he couldn't grab it. Theo stretched out on his tip toes, with Suhaan holding him for balance. Still no good.

'This isn't working' Theo shook his head. Hannah came forward, 'Jack, and all of you, you need to swing, you need to get some momentum going and then Jack will be able to reach the spear, so work together' she instructed them.

It took them a few tries, at first, they were all swinging in different directions, but with Miss Maggie's guidance, they were finally all swinging and swaying at the same time, Jack had his arms out through the gaps in the net. He stretched, pushing against the ropes until they felt like they were almost cutting into him, he saw the spear, the net was moving towards it, he reached and yes! Finally! He managed to grab hold of it, Theo almost dropped it at his end, but he kept a tight grip. With Suhaan and Hannah's help, he managed to drag the net over to them. Holding on tight, he passed the dagger to Miss Maggie, who quickly managed to make a cut in the rope, then another cut and another until they had a hole big enough for them to wiggle through.

Miss Maggie was last, before she came out Theo stopped her, 'Hold on Miss, we need the rope so I need you to cut off as much of it as you can from the top and jump with it.' Miss Maggie looked confused, but she didn't question it, figuring they needed it for a good reason.

Once all of them were out of the net, and they had as much of the net as Miss Maggie was able to cut off, Theo led them down the stairs, back toward the treasure room.

'Ok so don't freak out when you get down there, Theodore is a proper for real ghost. Like you can stick your hand through him type of Casper ghost, and he's friendly, so just don't freak,' he reminded them.

Theodore was standing away from the stairs this time, his hands behind his back, as the new lot came in, he tipped his ghostly hat at them, 'Good something, not sure if it's morning, afternoon, evening or night' he told them all.

Theo looked over at them to see how they were taking this all in, the kids all seemed ok, it was Miss Maggie he was worried about, her eyes were huge, her face had gone super pale. She just stared at Theodore. Simon, Sarah and Jack were running about picking up coins and throwing them, but Miss Maggie just kept still, her eyes nervously going to Theodore every now and then.

'What do you plan to do with that then boy' he asked Theo nodding towards the rope. 'I figured we can make a rope ladder, climb out and go back, try another way maybe, I can't just sit here and do nothing, especially since returning the shield didn't work.' Miss Maggie seemed to break out of her fright over Theodore being a ghost, 'What happened with the shield?' she asked.

Hannah jumped in with the explanation, 'We had a theory, that since we had the shield that belonged here, maybe returning it to its rightful place would somehow return us to our rightful place. But that theory was a bust, so now we either play pretend tea party with Theodore or look for another way out' she crossed her arms over her chest as she finished, waiting to see what Miss Maggie would say.

It wasn't Miss Maggie who spoke up though, it was Sarah. 'Hang about guys,' she came to stand next to Hannah, 'Do even replicas need to be returned do you think?' she asked them all, looking form Theo to Suhaan, then Hannah and finally to Theodore. She was a bit hesitant to make eye contact with Theodore, especially when he glitched, it made her nervous.

Theo turned to Sarah, 'What are you talking about?' he frowned as he asked. Sarah took off her backpack and reached into it, she took out a necklace – it was a stunning necklace. It had a central pendant that was shaped like a falcon clutching an ankh, he got it, it was a play on the cursed Pharaohs name, Nakth -Ankh. Around the pendant were small golden scarabs whose wings were encrusted with emeralds. The collar of the necklace was made from gold so smooth it looked liquid, how on earth had Sarah convinced herself this was a replica thought Theo.

Theodore floated closer to Sarah, he cleared his throat dramatically, 'My dear' he said, 'That is no replica.'

Sarah blinked, 'Really? It's not a fake? Huh, I thought it was' she replied, not that impressed by it being the real thing.

'You young lady, are holding the Eye of Eternity, the ceremonial necklace that the cursed one had commissioned and made especially for himself upon declaring himself the new Pharaoh. Suffice to say no one from that time wanted anything to do with this piece of self indulgence.'

Sarah's eyes widened, 'What. You mean to say I was carrying something that belonged to a real Pharaoh? Like real royalty, wow omg.'

Theodore gave her a quizzical look, not understanding everything she was saying, he floated away, these children and their speech gave him a headache, worse than when they shrieked at him.

'So… what does that mean for us?' Suhaan asked, his tone cautious. Theo straightened up, his eyes suddenly looking alive with purpose, 'It means we might still have a shot at going home, it means we just have to return this ugly necklace to its rightful place' he told Suhaan flinging an arm over his friend's shoulder. 'It also means, we need to get cracking making that ladder.' Miss Maggie looked to Theodore, he nodded in approval, 'The boy's right, you still have a chance, you just need to return the necklace to where I took it from, which was from the top of the Sarcophagus.'

Miss Maggie looked a bit annoyed, 'Why can't you just float over there and put it back yourself, seeing as you took it,' she asked him. Suhaan jumped in to answer, 'We kind of covered this while you were hanging around in the net, he can't touch any of the treasure, the curse you know.' He told her with a shrug of his shoulders.

The group wasted no time in gathering around the net, Theo and Suhaan went and collected some spears. 'Alright,' Theo began, 'We need the ladder to reach up there' he said, pointing to the gaping hole they had fallen through. Suhaan and Jack worked alongside Theo, lining up the spears in pairs to form the sides, they then cut the net into small lengths to tie the spears together. Miss Maggie helped them tie the knots, as the rope needed to hold their weight, so the knots had to be very secure.

They placed the spears tip down, so the tips could dig into the ground, and slowly lifted their makeshift ladder, it was a bit longer than they needed, which was fine. They stood there admiring their handiwork, 'Alright, I'll go first, then you all follow behind' he instructed. Thoe turned to Theodore, who stood apart from the group, his ghostly form shimmering in and out. 'If this works, we're getting out of here.' Theodore nodded, he had enjoyed having some company, but he knew he couldn't be selfish and expect them to remain here.

Theo swallowed a sudden lump in his throat, 'It was, I didn't,' he struggled to find the right words. 'Look, my grandpa speaks a lot about you, so it was really cool to get to meet you. If this works, I won't forget you, I'll find a way to let you be free, well your ghostly spirit to be released from here at least.' Theo and Theodore shared a smile, Theodore felt a pain in his ghostly chest, Theo was older than he had left Harold when he went on his expedition, yet here was a great example of how well Harold must have turned out, he wished he hadn't missed that.

'You take care kid, be careful out there, and it was a real pleasure meeting you, the best

Theodore Hawthorne out of all the ones I know,' he told Theo, Theo laughed, 'You only know two' he pointed out. Theodore nodded and tipped his hat to Theo.

Chapter fourteen

Theo reached the top of the makeshift ladder, gripping the last rung as he pulled himself onto the uneven, previously broken floor of this small room, if you could call it that. He steadied himself, then pushed up as much as he could to make space for Suhaan, who stood next to him, both of them looking into the room of the flying spears. Not relishing having to go through that again.

'Come on up guys' Theo called to the rest. One by one the others joined Suhaan and Theo in the cramped space.

'This is worse than the lunch queue at school' complained Jack. 'Stop talking about food, It's making me hungry' Simon told him. Theo gestured for them all to be quiet, 'Listen guys, this room here, we crossed it, it's not easy, but clearly it's possible. You have to step on the correct slabs cos if you don't then arrows or spears will shoot out of the walls at you,' he warned. Theo turned to face the deadly room, he was about to step into it, when there was a bit of jostle for more space, the motion moved and jostled everyone which in turn knocked Theo off his feet and he landed with a thud into the room, on the incorrect slab. He knew what was coming, so he tried to get as flat as he could while balancing just on his butt, arms and legs spread out low to the floor, kind of like Tom Cruise in his Mission Impossible pose, but the other way round. The sounds of creaking came and followed by that a spear shout of the wall, but luckily due to his quick thinking, it flew right over him, missing him by centimetres. Phew, that could have been so bad.

Suhaan reached out to help him get on his feet, Theo looked at his group, his eyes very serious, just like his tone. 'Guys, you have to not mess around, did you see what happened, instead of hitting the wall the spear can very easily hit one of us, so please, be careful about yourself and each other' he told them. It was Jack who spoke up very quietly, 'I'm sorry Theo, I was trying to get some space and…' he trailed off. 'Just go slow and be careful' Theo told him,' turning around to pick out the next slab to step on.

Everyone watched very carefully, keeping track of the steps, Suhaan followed him, as soon as Theo stepped off a slab, Suhaan stepped on it, and behind him was Miss Maggie, then Simon, Sarah, Jack and Hannah finished off their line. Luckily everyone was very careful after that initial fright, and there were no more accidents.

It felt like they had all been holding their breath, too scared to even breathe as they navigated that booby trapped room. Once they all made it through, they stood there, enjoying their small success, a shared thrill buzzed through them all.

'I can't believe we made it through there' Sarah gave a little laugh as she spoke, 'I was for sure nearly falling over my own feet so many times.'

Miss Maggie looked around at them all, 'I hope you all know I am really proud of how well you have been working together for this. I just wish it was under better circumstances.'

'When we make it back, someone needs to give us badges that say I survived the flying spears of doom, the hanging net, the ghost of trapped treasures and everything else' Simon added, laughing. Even Theo smiled at that one, but then his smile dropped. 'Guys, sorry to put a stop to us celebrating, but we're not done, we still need to go put the necklace back,' he told them, Miss Maggie, Jack, Simon and Sarah turned to look at the passage way that had no inscription, only endless darkness welcoming them.

Miss Maggie got her phone ready again, it didn't have much charge left and the torch seemed a bit dimmer than before. The little corridor felt even tighter than before as they all made their way through, Theo was at the front with Miss Maggie behind him, holding her phone up above his head, which was letting him see the way. Slowly and quietly they all entered the room.

The dim phone torch barely reached the edges of the chamber, casting spooky shadows everywhere. Theo, Suhaan and Hannah had not seen the sarcophagus before, they stood there taking in the huge size of it in the middle of the room on the sunken floor.

Miss Maggie, who wasn't as scared this time, looked around the room, 'Look over there kids, there's a door in the corner, an exit,' she pointed out to them all. 'Listen, here's what we'll do, you all head towards the exit, while I return the necklace, that way you will be close enough to get out if the tricksy tomb starts to close the walls on us again' she told them, by now getting quite used to expecting something to keep going wrong.

'It's a good plan Miss Maggie, but I think I should be the one to return the necklace, only because it was my great-grand-father who removed it from here' he told her. 'He has a good point Miss, what if it needs to be like for like, and he is technically Theodore Hawthorne' Hannah added.

Miss Maggie thought it over, the kids did have a point, and if they only had one go at escaping she didn't want to risk ruining it in any way at all. 'Ok,' she nodded at Theo, 'We do it your way, we will all be over there ready to run if anything starts to close on us, you be careful' she told him. Theo grabbed hold of Suhaan's hand as he was passing him, 'Be ready to run if anything starts going crazy' he told him, Suhaan nodded and followed the others towards the exit. Sarah was last, she paused to take the necklace out of her bag and hand it to Theo, 'Be careful Theo' she told him and joined everyone else.

Theo stood at the edge of the three massive stone steps leading down to the sarcophagus. Each step was really big, it was more of a jump down than a step down for Theo. Swallowing the lump in his throat, Theo hopped down the first step, then the second, he wiped the sweat off his face with the one hand he had free. How was he sweating in this cold room? Taking a few steadying breaths, Theo hopped down the final step, his knees felt a bit wobbly with the last jump, but he was ok.

Miss Maggie's light was barely reaching the sarcophagus now, he looked at the carvings on the side, trying not to touch the stone coffin at all he tip toed to reach up and place the necklace. He couldn't get a good look so he just placed it as best he could, 'Theo there are markings on where the necklace needs to go, you need to push it all up a bit' Miss Maggie called out to him. He looked over to see Miss Maggie, Simon and Suhaan standing near the doorway, all looking as nervous as he felt.

Theo stepped away for a second, he wiped his hands on his jumper, then got as close to the sarcophagus as he could, he was now pressed up against the cold stone, he felt around the top to feel the grooves of where the necklace had to go and pulled it up, then straightened it out until it was all sitting in place as it should be. An ominous rumble shook the room. 'Here we go again' Theo shouted out above the groaning noise in the room, the walls trembled, dust and debris started falling from the ceiling, but it was the exit door that started to shudder and move, 'Uh guys, another booby trap, run!' shouted Suhaan, turning for the doorway.

Miss Maggie turned and knocked into Suhaan, causing them both to trip and fall, her phone scattered from her hand, sending the room into darkness.

Theo had been scrambling up the final step when the room went dark, he lost his footing and fell hard on his ankle. Pain shot through his entire foot, 'AARGH!' he cried out.' 'What's happened?' Simon's voice drifted through the darkness. 'I've hurt my foot, and I can't see anything' Theo called out. He was feeling scared as he could hear the grinding that let him know the door was closing, he didn't want to be stuck here in this room forever with that thing. His breathing was getting shallow just thinking about it, when he felt something touch him.

'Ahhhhh!' he yelped in fright. 'Be quiet and give me your arm,' It was Simon, Simon had come in the dark to help him. He felt Simon put his arm over Simon's shoulders and then Simon supported Theo to scramble up the step. Miss Maggie had found her phone and managed to turn the light back on, 'Hurry boys, Hurry!,' she called as she went through the closing doorway, Theo could see it was coming down from the top this time, as they approached the half shut door, Simon practically threw Theo through the gap and then slid under it himself just in time.

'Keep moving' Miss Maggie shouted to everyone, as the grinding noise continued, she was still reliving the moment when the previous room had closed in on them, so she didn't want to stop moving until the noise stopped.

Following the tunnel through they realised it led back to the central point, coughing and covered in dust they looked at each other, not knowing what to expect. Simon had helped Theo all the way out, now he finally let Theo sit on the floor, removing his arm from around his own shoulders.

Suhaan and Hannah came rushing towards

Theo and Simon, 'Are you guys alright? That was so brave' Hannah told Simon. Suhaan threw his arms around Simon, surprising him. 'Thanks for saving my best friend' he said, his voice was all choked up.

'Yeah, thanks man for coming back for me' Theo told him gratefully.

Simon shifted awkwardly, his ears turning red from the attention, 'It's no big deal' he mumbled.

'It is a big deal, Theo told him, 'I couldn't, I was, basically I owe you,' Theo finally managed.

Simon shrugged again trying to downplay it all. 'Couldn't let you get turned into mummy food could I?' he quipped with a small grin.

They sat in silence for a moment, catching their breath. The relief of escaping alive quickly gave way to disappointment.

Jack looked down at himself and then around at the tomb walls, 'We're still here. Why are we still here?'

'Maybe it wasn't enough. Maybe we are stuck like Theodore until all the pieces are returned.' Sarah sounded really sad as she spoke.

'Maybe we should head back to the treasure room, it seemed the safest,' Theo suggested to the group.

Before anyone could respond, the air in the chamber shifted. It started as a faint whisper, a soft breeze that passed over all of them.

'It's happening again', Theo whispered, he was really excited this time, he looked at the others who were noticing the gathering dust that had started to spin and spiral in the air.

The tornado swelled, filling the little room with a deafening hum. The walls of the tomb seemed to vibrate; the eerie glow of the hieroglyphs flickered. They had to shield their eyes and faces as the tornado grew more fierce, 'Hold on to each other!' Miss Maggie yelled at them over the noise. Theo reached out to Hannah and Simon who were closest to him, but before he could reach their hands there was a blast of energy in the room and then darkness.

Chapter fifteen

Theo felt like he was waking up from a sleep, but he could feel the cold hard floor against his face. There was no sand grit in his eyes this time. For a horrible minute he wasn't sure if he had just been dreaming, but then he saw the rest of his group, also slowly waking and looking around.

'That did all happen right, right?' Suhaan asked next to him, 'Like I didn't fall asleep and have some weird dream did I?'

'If you did then so did I' Hannah told him, 'And me', 'Me too', 'And me' the others all answered as they slowly got to their feet.

Theo sat up and glanced around the little room. The artifacts glimmered innocently under the lights, as if they weren't part of some time travelling curse. We can't tell anyone about this,' Theo said, breaking the silence. 'No kidding,' Simon muttered, brushing sand from his shirt. 'Can you imagine if we tried to say 'Hey, guess what? We just got back from ancient Egypt after battling curses and booby traps.' They'd lock us up in no time.' Hannah nodded, 'He's right. No one would believe us anyway.'

Miss Maggie brushed off her clothes, still a bit shaken, 'Even if they did, it would only make things worse. People would swarm this place, trying to steal the artifacts for themselves, no good would come of it.'

The truth of her words sunk in, people would want to steal more artifacts from that place, and who knew what other dangers might be released if it continued? No, the world couldn't find out about the cursed tomb. Too much was at stake.

'So, it's up to us to keep this a secret,' Theo said, his voice steady. 'I have to return the rest of the artifacts. All of them. If I don't, the curse will keep Theodore's ghost prisoner, and Theodore—' He stopped, his throat tightening at the memory of Theodore's final words. 'We can't leave him trapped like that,' Hannah finished for him. Simon crossed his arms. 'Well, if you're going back in there, you're not doing it alone. I'm coming too.'

'Same,' Suhaan added, adjusting his glasses. 'You'll need all the help you can get. 'Count me in,' Sarah said, surprising everyone. 'I mean, I'm not going to lie—I'm terrified. But we've already come this far. And it feels wrong to not help you help Theodore, who helped us get back, if you see what I mean' she gestured with her hands as she spoke, everyone got what she meant. Theodore had helped them, and it felt mean to let him hang around by himself as a ghost.

Miss Maggie sighed, her expression softening. 'Well, I can't let you kids do this without an adult present, can I?' Theo smiled at them all, his heart swelling with gratitude. 'Thanks, everyone. I mean it.'

Miss Maggie looked down at her watch then, 'Oh my goodness, it's 5pm, we need to go meet the rest of the class quickly.'

As they hurried to leave, Gary appeared in the gallery, looking annoyed. 'What are you all doing here? Didn't you see the sign? Out! Now, before you get us all in trouble!' he almost shouted at them.

Theo exchanged amused glances with all his friends, because that's what they were now, well friends and 1 teacher. They all started giggling at the thought of the kind of trouble they had just survived. Gary looked at them all as if they had gone a bit mad, he didn't understand why they all started giggling, but at least they left like he asked.

A few days later, the group gathered inside the museum and when no one was looking, they snuck into the gallery. This time, they weren't alone. Grandpa Harold stood with them, and Hannah had brought along Kacey, the one person she had told. As she explained, that was her best friend in the whole world, and they told each other everything.

'So, let me go over this one more time,' Harold said, scratching his beard. 'You're saying these artifacts are cursed, and we need to return them to their rightful places?'

'Exactly,' Theo said. 'And you're telling me you think this will release the curse on my father, who is a ghost and just hanging around, in a chamber of treasures in ancient Egypt,' Harold asked.

Theo nodded, 'yep, that's exactly it'

'Ok, let's do this then' Harold said. They had planned out which order to collect all the items, everyone was wearing gloves, as they figured that the curse had got triggered by Theo touching it without gloves or because he too was a Theodore Hawthorne, but just to be safe they let Theo pick only the last item, which was a spear.

Sand appeared on the gallery floor, and started swirling, but this time they weren't afraid, this time they were a bit better prepared, they all had bags with essentials like torches, a first aid kit, rope, and a folding lightweight ladder. Theo looked at everyone, 'Everyone ready?' he asked.

'Ready as we'll ever be,' Simon said, adjusting the strap of his bag.

The wind picked up, swirling sand turning into a tornado. The group huddled closer as the storm intensified, the gallery fading into a blur of flickering light.

The End

ABOUT THE AUTHOR

Born and raised in London, my love for reading and history started from an early age. I had always wanted to write my own stories but never seemed to find the time. 2023 was a year for making changes, and I finally finished and published my first book that year, from then finding the time hasn't been the problem, the issue is now which story do I want to tell next.

You can find my other works at farahuddin.com, where you can also find out how to contact me.

Printed in Great Britain
by Amazon